ANGLO-WELSH LITERATURE · An Illustrated History

Volume Four in the series

The Illustrated History of the Literatures of Wales.

edited by

Bedwyr Lewis Jones

ANGLO~WELSH LITERATURE · An Illustrated History

Roland Mathias

POETRY WALES PRESS
1987

POETRY WALES PRESS
56 PARCAU AVENUE, BRIDGEND, MID GLAMORGAN

British Library Cataloguing in Publication Data

Mathias, Roland
Anglo-Welsh literature: an illustrated history.
— (Illustrated history of the literatures of Wales; v.4)
1. English literature — Welsh authors — History and criticism
I. Title II. Series
820.9'9429   PR8951

ISBN 0-907476-64-3

Cover Design by Jeane Rees

Cover Illustration: The Harvesters by Brenda Chamberlain
From the collection of Mrs Joan Brinley Rees, photograph by Rosie Waite.

The publisher acknowledges the financial support of the Welsh Arts Council

Printed in 11 point Times
by
D. Brown & Sons Ltd, Bridgend

Contents

Illustrations

1. Offa's Dyke, near Knighton
2. Laugharne Castle, on the estuary of the Taf
3. Jesus College, Oxford
4. The Language Clause from the Act of Union, 1536
5. Ruthin: An Elizabethan Grammar School.
6. David Baker, re-establisher of the Benedictine Order in Britain.
7. Cefn Brith, birthplace of John Penry
8. John Dee
9. Humphrey Llwyd's Map of Wales, 1573
10. Thomas Pennant
11. *The Blessedness of Brytaine*
12. John Davies of Hereford
13. St. Donat's Castle
14. 'The Matchless Orinda'
15. Henry Vaughan's *Olor Iscanus*
16. Brecknock Priory, 1793
17. James Howell
18. William Williams, Pantycelyn.
19. The Reverend William Thomas: *Islwyn*
20. Lewis Morris: *Llewelyn Ddu o Fôn*
21. *Iolo Morganwg* (Edward Williams)
22. Richard Llwyd, 'The Bard of Snowdon'
23. Sir Charles Hanbury-Williams
24. Nanteos, later the home of George Powell.
25. A View of Brecon
26. Anna Williams
27. 'Children Cutting Out Paper People'
28. 'Ann of Swansea' (Julia Ann Hatton)
29. 'Swansea Bay' by A. Wilson
30. Felicia Hemans
31. Gerard Manley Hopkins as a boy
32. Lady Charlotte Guest
33. John Dyer, poet and artist
34. Grongar Hill.
35. Evan Lloyd, cleric and satirist
36. Sir Lewis Morris
37. Robert Owen's Ideal Village, Orbiston, Lanarkshire
38. An Archdruid in his Judicial Habit
39. Rees Gronow
40. Thomas Love Peacock
41. Sker House, on the Glamorgan coast
42. 'Twm Sion Catti Offering a Horse for Sale at Llandovery Fair'
43. Mallt Williams
44. *The Red Dragon*

Author's Note

My first and most obvious debt is to Raymond Garlick's pioneering work, *An Introduction to Anglo-Welsh Literature* (1970). Without this as guide, I should have been involved with many more months of enquiry and research.

I am grateful, too, to Patrick Thomas for notes on seventeenth century writers like William Harbert and Hugh Holland and for a pre-publication sight of his article on the nineteenth century versifier George Thomas of Llandyssil.

Sally Roberts Jones provided me with a substantial list of early Anglo-Welsh novels compiled from her own library, a list of which space, unfortunately, permitted only a very selective use.

I owe my knowledge of the writings of Clifford King to the interest of the late Onfel Thomas, who lent me a copy of *To the Ocean, To Greece*.

In thanking all these, I must make it plain that they are not responsible either for my evaluations of individual writers or for the groupings or movements that I suggest. My mistakes, constructively or otherwise, are my own.

I The Arrival of English

Of the two languages of Wales, Welsh was undoubtedly the earlier arrival. Whether it came in, in its most primitive or Celtic or Indo-European form, with the Beaker Folk about 1900 B.C. or considerably later with the incursion of the first Iron Age A Celts in the mid-eighth century B.C. is still matter for argument. And there is not much greater certainty about the time of arrival of the English language within Wales's borders. But that it was considerably earlier than used commonly to be believed now seems very likely. Place-name evidence suggests that Mercian settlers had entered the valleys of the Lugg, the Arrow and the Wye earlier than the end of the eighth century A.D. when King Offa built his Dyke, and almost certainly much of Herefordshire, the Teme valley in Worcestershire, eastern Radnorshire and Breconshire (anachronistically named territorial areas, of course) constituted regions of mixed Welsh-speaking and English-speaking settlements which remained peaceably contiguous into Norman times. The relative weakness of the Welsh language in the parts of the Welsh counties named, and perhaps in southern Montgomeryshire too, may be traced to this long-standing situation, which in the seventeenth century made possible the proselytisation of Welshmen by monoglot English-speaking evangelists of the Puritan persuasion. It was no accident that the origins of Dissent in Wales are to be found in places like Brampton Bryan, the home of the Harleys, Llanfair Waterdine, a favourite preaching station, and Cnwclas, the birthplace of Vavasor Powell.

1. Offa's Dyke, near Knighton

But long before this English had established itself in much less likely parts of Wales and in fashion more dramatic. In the winter of 1108-9 Henry I settled in Pembrokeshire a number of Flemings whose lands had been inundated. But *Anglia Transwallina* – Little England beyond Wales, as Camden was later to call the Flemish hundreds – could not have been created solely by Flemings (despite the facile repetitions of historians through the centuries). George Owen of Henllys, the Pembrokeshire antiquary of Elizabethan times, was of the much cannier opinion that the main bulk of the settlers came from England rather than Flanders, as indeed the *ton* endings to village names abundantly indicate. Almost nothing is known of this settlement, mysteriously marked off to the north by the Landsker ('mysteriously' because *Landsker* is a Norse word), but the eastern angle of it created by the southern coast and the Taf as it runs down from Whitland seems not to have been fully 'planted'. There was a Norman (subsequently English) castle and dependent borough at Laugharne, but a Welsh corridor taking in Llanddowror, Tavernspite and what is now called Red Roses ran across the Taf from Whitland down to the sea at Marros and Pendine. The linguistic complexity of the southern coastline (Welsh at Llansteffan, English at Laugharne, Welsh at Marros, English from Amroth westward) which has lingered into this century is deepened by the existence of another English-speaking region to the east of Carmarthen Bay – that is, the southern and major portion of the Gower peninsula – from the twelfth or thirteenth century onwards. About this, too, little or nothing is known: its area can be delineated clearly enough by place and field names, but the best guess so far about its cause and origin is that it likewise was 'planted' with English

2. Laugharne Castle, on the estuary of the Taf

settlers by the Norman lord of Swansea, who expected not only a better economic return from the Englishries of his feudal demesne but also a degree of protection against the Welshmen of the mountains to the north from an alien population whose own isolation would compel it to be faithful. Undoubtedly both the most southerly part of Pembrokeshire and the Gower peninsula subsequently attracted a few settlers from the ports of Somerset and Devon, with which a lively trade was conducted in centuries after the fifteenth, but by that time the presence of refugees from Ireland in great numbers (especially in Tenby and the regions surrounding it) had made irrevocably English in speech a large part of Wales's south-westerly promontory.

Meanwhile, smaller Englishries had been established by Norman lords who had built castles in the Usk, Wye and Monnow valleys: these were primarily economic in origin, set up to cultivate the fertile bottom land by the river, and they were, in the end, too small to survive linguistically against a Welsh background except in one or two places like Hay, where a considerable town population seems to have ensured the continuance of English. After the defeat of the last Prince of Gwynedd in 1284 the establishment of royal boroughs in North Wales – like Beaumaris, Caernarfon and Harlech – had an effect roughly similar. Towns in the South, like Brecon and Carmarthen, were preserves of English and, few as these were for a very long time, they confined commerce throughout Wales to alien hands. Indeed, the first kind of full-blooded Welshman to learn English was probably the would-be chapman or market trader.

A second class of English-learner was soon to emerge: the student. In seeking a

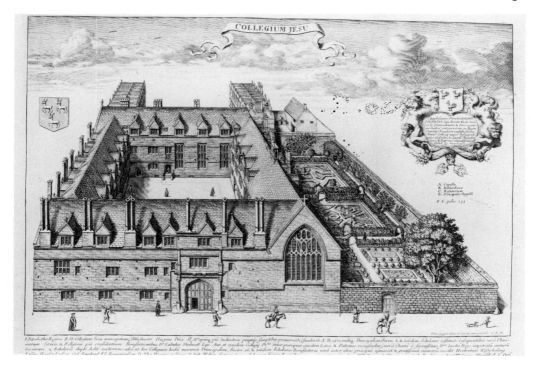

3. Jesus College, Oxford, from R. Loggan, *Oxonia Illustrata*, 1675

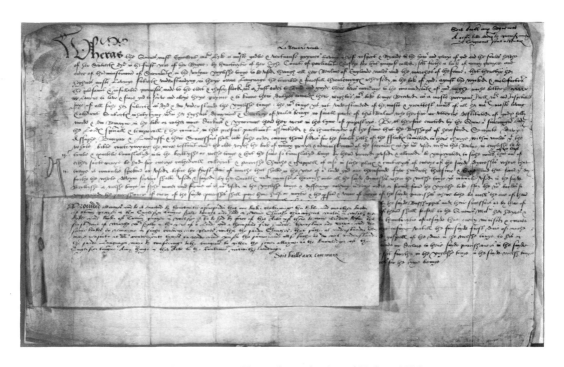

4. The Language Clause from the Act of Union, 1536

university he was compelled to go outside the confines of his own country (despite the hope of Griffith Yonge and the other clerical followers of Glyndŵr): he might go to Oxford (where Oriel was 'the Welsh College' before Jesus was founded in 1571), to Cambridge or across the sea to Padua or Paris.

English had been a requirement for office in Wales, whether royal or feudal, ever since the genuinely Norman element amongst the King's servants or amongst marcher barons had declined. But the number of Welshmen qualified for such office was small. The Acts of Union of 1536 and 1542, however, made it incumbent upon all who held judicial office to use the English language only. The effect of this upon judges of assize was negligible: it was a rule that merely reinforced fact. But now justices of the peace, sheriffs, escheators and other holders of legal office in Wales were similarly compelled to English. As a result, the gentry of the March counties in particular (nearness to the Court of the Marches at Ludlow being an important element in the receipt of information about legal opportunity) swelled the numbers of students at the rapidly growing Inns of Court, qualification at which was much more quickly obtained than at the universities. The chance of riches (for the holding of legal office was undoubtedly one of the likeliest ways of achieving them), the extension of personal and family power through office in Wales, the extensive network of relationships already existing with those collaterals who had left Wales with Henry Tudor in 1485 and had been rewarded with estates in England – all these factors brought the Welsh gentry, within two centuries from the Acts of Union, not merely to speak English but to regard English as the mark of their rank and title. From the earliest days of industrialisation, too,

5. An Elizabethan Grammar School. Gabriel Goodman's 'scholehouse', Ruthin, 1574

pioneer English families – like the Hanburys of Pontypool – regarded themselves as gentry in Wales and put their profits into land. The effect was, in some parts of Wales more than others, to create a landowning class that was totally anglicised and, where the estates were poorer or the population more strongly Welsh, to induce the absence (in England or elsewhere) of gentry who felt that their status demanded it.

Meanwhile, the foundation of the Grammar Schools, from the time of Henry VIII onwards, anglicised intelligent and ambitious boys from a lower class. Christ College, Brecon, granted a charter in 1541, had for one of its *raisons d'etre* the interpretation to its *alumni* of the statutes of the realm through the acquisition of English – an echo of the Act of 1536. If there were not many instances as specific as this – and instruction in class, it must be remembered, was through Latin – the general aim of the education offered was to equip pupils with the classical knowledge needed to enter and make a way in a cultured English society. Many of the boys who passed through these schools – Ruthin and Queen Elizabeth, Carmarthen, are other examples – having proceeded to university, never came back to Wales. The majority of those who did became clergymen of the Church of England.

Until the second quarter of the nineteenth century, then, only the most privileged and intelligent Welshmen (except those from English-speaking enclaves) had had the opportunity to learn English. But that language was associated in the public mind not merely with class and profession, but with social status, education and success in industry or commerce. Only religion, and that for a brief period in the later sixteenth century (in the heyday of Richard Davies, William Salesbury and William Morgan), made any particular claim for Welsh.

Those for whom English was the natural language in which to write (and they cannot, until after 1850, have comprised even ten per cent of the population of Wales) were therefore either gentlefolk born, or those whose natural intelligence had been fortunately matched with educational opportunity, or inhabitants of South Pembrokeshire, Gower, a few royal boroughs and certain areas in the middle of the March, or such people as chapmen, drovers, merchants and students at universities whose occupation carried them to England and farther afield. It is perhaps remarkable that such a high proportion of the nation's intelligence produced, in literary terms, so little of value. But it must be remembered that the drain of that intelligence into appointments and enterprises in England was always high. Most of the first writers in English, as we shall see, were 'men of affairs'. Of those clergy who held incumbencies in Wales, a few devoted themselves to writing in Welsh. For the remaining English-speakers, while the determining factor was undoubtedly the language of their education, a certain awkwardness or ambivalence in their attitude to locality and Wales possibly prevented creativity and it needed a political, economic or spiritual crisis, as in the cases of the notable exceptions Henry Vaughan and John Dyer, to compel them to expression. There were, however, some reasons other than those of crisis which led a few whose natural or better language was Welsh to undertake part of their writing in English – reasons, usually though not always, of an evangelical nature, operative from the time of the Puritan Revolution onwards.

It needs to be made clear that the term 'Anglo-Welsh', as it is used in the pages following, has a literary connotation quite separate from that which it might bear in other contexts. Literarily, it implies no mixture of blood (though that may happen), no half-and-halfing, no special *rapprochement* with England or its interests: it describes those writers who by birth or strong family derivation and residence were Welsh but who, whether from necessity or choice, wrote in English. Our primary interest then (until the twentieth century) will be devoted to those who, whatever their more common choice of language, wrote at some time creatively in English.

II First Works in English

After what has been written so far, it should come as no surprise that the first poem in English is attributed to a student, Ieuan ap Hywel Swrdwal from the Cydewain district of Powys, who, while at Oxford about 1470, wrote an *awdl* to the Virgin Mary. But this was reputedly a *boast* poem, a one-off (as is said too often nowadays), composed, it is true, of English words but spelled in Welsh and put together with an intricacy which no English poet of the time could wish to imitate. Amongst the stanzas which best show the strangeness of the combination is the short fifth (there are longer twelve-line stanzas later in the poem):

> Kwin od off owr God, owr geiding / mwdyr,
> maedyn notwythstanding,
> hwo wed syts wyth a ryts ring
> as God wod ddys gwd weding.

Some of the difficulty of this poem for the modern reader is attributable to the sibilant English (*ryts* for *rich*, for example) which a Welshman like Ieuan then spoke and some to contemporary English pronunciation (*mwdyr* is much closer to the older *moder* than to *mother*). But the motive for the poem's composition being temporary – a wager, as the tradition is – this first burst of English had no immediate or logical successors. Ieuan, son of a poet father, afterwards kept himself to Welsh.

Books in English by Welshmen in the early part of the sixteenth century (and it must not be forgotten how recently Caxton had brought the printing process to England) were almost inevitably those written by 'men of affairs', men, that is, who had left Wales and made their way in London or elsewhere. Indeed, too strong an insistence on 'creative writing' at this point would dismiss from these pages any concern at all with prose and reveal much of the poetry written as an extension into a creative medium of attitudes and concerns that were often so little personal as to be mere reflections of social status, current historical tradition and broad contemporary preoccupations. For this first period, then, little attempt will be made to discriminate: all writings of significance will be noted.

Perhaps the earliest book of all was an *Abridgement of the Common Law* by William Owen of Henllys in Pembrokeshire, father of the much better known George Owen. The edition which appeared in 1499 may have been his: those of 1521 and 1528 certainly were. John Gwynedd, the Oxford monk-musician from Castellmarch in Llŷn, one of whose songs, 'My love mourneth', was included in Wynkyn de Worde's *Bassus* in 1530, was at some time after 1533 writing and publishing theological answers, from the Catholic standpoint, to the controversial works of Tyndale's friend, John Frith. About the same time Richard Whitford, the Flintshire-born monk of Syon House, Isleworth, the friend of both Erasmus and More, was engaged on one or other of his sixteen devotional works, of which *A Dayly Exercyse and Experyence of Dethe* (1537) and *A Treatise of Patience* (1540) are perhaps the most memorable. In the same devotional tradition were the *Sancta Sophia* and *Holy Practices* of David Baker of Abergavenny, the re-establisher of the Benedictine Order in Britain: they were doubtless known to Benedictines of many generations, as to other Catholics, before they were finally published in 1657.

6. David Baker, re-establisher of the
Benedictine Order in Britain.
Drawing by G.P. Hardship

In the sixteenth century Wales produced, too, one of the most determined and notorious of the early Puritans. John Penry of Cefn-brith by Llangammarch, north of Eppynt, learned at Cambridge that unrelentingly earnest attitude that brought him unjustly to his death in 1593 as the much searched-for Martin Marprelate. "A poore young man borne and bredde in the mountaynes of Wales" and "the first since the last springing up of the Gospell in this latter age that publicly laboured to have the blessed seed thereof sowen in these barrayn mountaynes", as he described himself to Burleigh in the week before his death, he had published in 1587 *A Treatise containing the Aequity of an Humble Supplication* and two other pamphlets, an *Exhortation* and a *Supplication*, all three devoted to the spiritual needs of his country. It was, however, to be another forty years before the preaching of William Wroth, Walter Cradoc, William Erbery and Vavasor Powell invoked Penry's evangel again, and of these only Powell, the Fifth Monarchy man, published treatises more extended than the collected sermons demanded by admirers. Probably the anti-Puritan polemics of Alexander Griffith, the ejected vicar of Glasbury, in his *Strena Vavasoriensis* (1654), if less principled, are more to modern taste. In the case of Morgan Llwyd, another Puritan contemporary, religious enthusiasm made contact with a more literary tradition, but to that we shall recur in its rightful place. From the Quakers, whose impetus in Wales was largely English – despite the eloquence of John ap John – came in 1710 *An Account of the Convincement, Exercises, Services and Travels of that Ancient Servant of the Lord, Richard Davies* the kind of autobiographical record in English unique up to that time (the *Life of Edward, Lord Herbert of Cherbury* not being published till after 1737 and many now-known diaries not till much later than that).

The Church of England in Wales made much use of one book by a Welshman. Lewis Bayly's *The Practice of Piety* (1611), published five years before its author was appointed Bishop of Bangor, had by 1792 run to seventy-one editions.

7. Cefn Brith, the Eppynt farmhouse where John Penry was born

Plainly Welshmen, mostly by way of university, were making their way in the fields of religious discipline and controversy. More surprising is their appearance, ahead of any major concern at either Oxford or Cambridge, in the vanguard of writers on medicine, mathematics and science. Robert Recorde of Tenby, in the course of a career as court physician, comptroller of the royal mint and surveyor of mines, wrote what were the first treatises in English on arithmetic, algebra and geometry. *The Grounde of Artes* (1540), *The Pathway to Knowledge* (1551) and *The Whetstone of Witte* (1557) were many times reprinted. The first of these, augmented in 1561 by John Dee, who became the *magus* of the Elizabethan age, went through no fewer than twenty-six editions by 1662. In 1570 the first English *Euclid* was translated by Sir Henry Billingsley, later Lord Mayor of London but also of Penhow Castle in Gwent, an associate of Dee's in their common plan to make mathematical and scientific knowledge available in the vernacular, and Dee contributed a Mathematical Preface. The contribution of these Welshmen in this field was the most significant of its time. The much later works of Eugenius Philalethes – Thomas Vaughan of Scethrog (twin brother of the poet Henry Vaughan), who ended his career as one of the very earliest state scientists – consisted of seven alchemical treatises in the Rosicrucian tradition and two polemics against Henry More, all of them published between 1650 and 1656.

David Rowland's *A Comfortable Aid for Scholars* (1578), intended for students of Greek and Latin, and Lewis Roberts's *The Merchantes Mappe of Commerce* (1638) and *The Treasure of Trafficke* (1640), the latter a work on political economy, indicate other directions in which Welshmen had made some way. The military tradition of Gwent, though essentially one of practice rather than theory, nevertheless elicited from that daring soldier Sir Roger Williams of Penrhos (the probable model for Shakespeare's Fluellen) *A Brief Discourse of War* (1590) and two other books which

8. John Dee, *magus* of Elizabeth's reign

are largely military narrative. The *Military Memoirs* of Captain John Gwynne, who fought beside Montrose in the Civil War, were not published till 1822, when Sir Walter Scott edited them, but *Most Approved and Long experienced Water-Workes...*, an odd farrago by the ex-military man Rowland Vaughan of New Court in the Golden Valley, certainly did appear in 1610 – with a promise to repay each owner of a copy the sum of forty shillings in five years' time. Ostensibly about agriculture, this was an early example of a capital-raising publication (and there have been few as colourful), in which intention was glossed as already-existing achievement.

The study of medicine stood at the crossroads of knowledge (as we have seen in the case of Robert Recorde, whose *The Urinal of Physics* (1547) did not prevent its author from shaping popular mathematics), its own rudimentary nature inviting entry by practitioners of other disciplines. Thus the medical treatise *Organon Salutis* (1657), which ran to three editions, was the work of Walter Rumsey of Llanover, a lawyer, and Humphrey Llwyd of Denbigh, beginning with medicine and science, ventured into history (translating Caradoc of Llancarfan's chronicle into English and enlarging Sir John Price's *Description of Cambria*); he finally earned himself the most individual mark of all as the provider of maps of England and Wales for the supplement to the *Theatrum Orbis Terrarum* (1573) of Abraham Ortelius, the Antwerp atlas-maker.

The largest single group of those who wrote in English in the sixteenth and seventeenth centuries, however, was that of the historians, many of whom, like Llwyd and David Powel of Ruabon, had been educated at Oxford and were aware of the contemporary achievement of English historians and antiquaries. Llwyd and Powel responded, as did Sir John Price in Latin, to Polydore Vergil's attack on the credibility of Geoffrey of Monmouth's *History of the Kings of Britain*. The influence and standing of Camden, who published *Britannia* in 1586, inspired George Owen of Henllys who completed his *Description of Penbrockshire* in 1603, Rice Merrick, whose *Morganiae Archaiographia: a Booke of Glamorganshire Antiquities* was still being added to at the author's death in 1586-7, and probably Sir John Wynn, whose *The History of the Gwydir Family* was not published until 1770. As the Acts of Union had promised, there

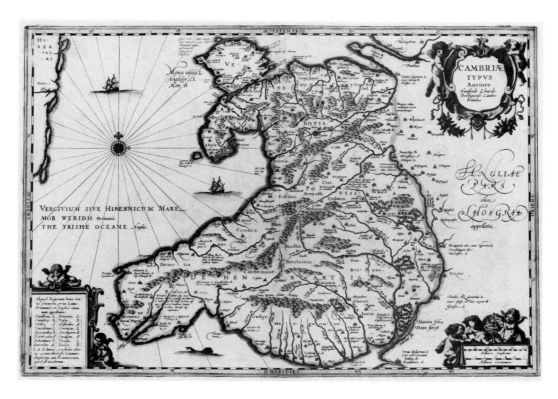

9. Humphrey Llwyd's Map of Wales, 1573

was an intellectual opportunity for Welshmen – in English – and the response from historians was more unreasoningly patriotic than might have been expected. John Lewis of Llynwene's *The History of Great Britain...til the Death of Cadwaladr*, written in the early years of James I's reign, would accept none of Polydore Vergil's criticisms and David Powel's *Historie of Cambria* (1584) influenced writers on Welsh history for a period longer than it deserved. There are glimpses, too, of the sentimental patronage of Lord Burleigh, for whom Sir Edward Stradling of St. Donat's put on record before 1571 the tall story of the conquest of Glamorgan by Fitzhamon and his twelve knights. Norman-Welsh fiction, like Geoffrey's *History*, was still a powerful driving force amongst the Welsh. Even the Wiltshire-born John Aubrey, two generations away from Wales, felt some of the impulse: he was the first to make the Romantic, but historically incorrect, association of the Druids with the building of Stonehenge.

It is impossible, in a disquisition as brief as this, to follow much further either the Welshmen who disseminated knowledge in general or the Welsh historians in particular. The latter were especially numerous in later centuries, some of them possessing a basis of local knowledge and research that was sound for its time, as with Henry Rowlands, who published *Mona Antiqua Restaurata* in 1723. Others, such as Rowland Jones with his *The Circles of Gomer* (1771), and Edward Davies, with his *The Mythology and Rites of the British Druids* (1809), were carried away by the more lunatic tides of Romanticism. The travellers, of whom only a few, like Thomas Pennant

10. Thomas Pennant: portrait by Gainsborough

(whose *Tours in Wales* is still eminently worth reading), were Welshmen, began to provide a more particular and apparently objective basis for local history, and there followed, within a few years of each other (c.1805-10) Richard Fenton's *A Historical Tour through Pembrokeshire*, Samuel Rush Meyrick's *History and Antiquities of the County of Cardigan* and Theophilus Jones's *History of the County of Brecknock*.

III Early Poetry: The Sixteenth and Seventeenth Centuries

The literary field proper, which is our chief concern, is never entirely separated from the historical, least of all when the latter is sown with Romantic tradition, and there are a number of instances where a writer ploughs both. Fenton, for instance, was a poet as well as a historian, and with Iolo Morganwg (for whom history was more a planted garden than a field) overmastering interest made no distinctions. In terms of the Anglo-Welsh categories already suggested, it is worth noticing that Rowlands and 'Celtic' Davies were clerics (the latter from already anglicised Radnorshire), that Rowland Jones, Fenton, Meyrick and Theophilus Jones were all lawyers – the first three with long periods of their lives spent in London, the last with very close archidiaconal associations – and that Pennant was an Oxford-educated member of an anglicised gentry family from Flintshire. Iolo the stonemason, in origin an English-speaker from the linguistically uncertain Vale of Glamorgan, defies social categorisation as such an eccentric genius should.

The field of creative writing – which means, for the best part of three centuries from 1470, verse only – was barer and much less exciting. Undoubtedly a great deal of what was written during those three centuries has never, in modern times, been available in print and current research may well prove untrue such generalisations as can now be made. But what we can discern of the verse written in the sixteenth century follows the same pattern as that drawn by the historians, that of an acceptance of the 'opportunity' to Welshmen afforded by the Acts of Union and the demonstration, in English, of a balancing pride in Wales as the original provider, not merely of the House of Tudor but of a monarchy descended from Brutus the Trojan. The prevalence of this 'seniority theme' was the legacy of that enormously influential historical fiction, Geoffrey of Monmouth's *Historia Regum Britanniae* (1136) and its popularity, of course, reflects the status of the writers: they were either at Court or somewhere within the circle of patronage.

Two anonymous poems, until recently hidden in the Bodleian manuscript known as Rawlinson MS C 813, are concerned with the death in 1521 of Sir Gruffydd ap Rhys, son to the better-known Rhys ap Thomas, lord of Dinefwr. Sir Gruffydd was a courtier-gentleman whose last appearance of note may have been at the Field of the Cloth of Gold in 1520. The supposed death-soliloquy of the "griffith" who came flying over the author's head from "the mountains of Wales by south west", strikes the appropriately loyal note:

> Farewell England! Farewell Wales!
> I take my leave now at this tide.
> Farewell Calais and English Pales!
> Farewell King Henry! I may not abide,
> Death hath me lanced into the side.
> Farewell knighthood, farewell chivalry!
> Of the courteous court farewell good company!

The conspectus of ideas here obviously embraces the Arthurian tradition in its Frenchified form and the splendid union of England and Wales in the person of a still-unsullied Tudor monarch.

But sixty years later there was little change, partly, one supposes, because the reign of Elizabeth, still surrounded personally by Welsh men and women, was a demonstrable glory in which the contemporary patriotism, even imperialism, compelled poets to share, and partly because the origins and interests of those poets were still as restricted as they had ever been. Maurice Kyffin of Oswestry, who wrote in Welsh as well as English, was not merely a disciple of John Dee but a royal officer in the Netherlands and Ireland. His chief work in Welsh was a translation of Bishop Jewel's *Apologia* for the doctrinal compromise represented by the Church of England. In English *The Blessedness of Brytaine* (1587) was a poem in praise of Queen Elizabeth:

> Ye Bryttish Poets, Repeat in Royall Song,
> (With waightie woords, used in King Arthurs daies)
> Th' Imperiall Stock, from whence your Queene hath sprong;
> Enstall in verse your Princesse lasting prayes:
> Pencerddiaid, play on Auncient Harp, and Crowde:
> Atceiniad, sing her prayses pearcing lowd.

This stanza, it should be added, in that it beckons *Wales*, does not reflect adequately the *general* nature of the command to tribute. But Geoffrey's *History*, it is plain, had lost nothing of its power, except perhaps for recusants whose desperate responses to persecution left little time for verse. In this vein the poets were little more than a less informative echo of Arthur Kelton's *A Commendacion of Welshmen* (1546), in whose more execrable doggerel the term 'Welshman' plainly extended not much further than the Tudors and those from Wales who were about them at Court.

More can be learned about Wales, indeed, from the book-length poem of another Shrewsbury man, Thomas Churchyard. His *Worthines of Wales* (1587), which reveals

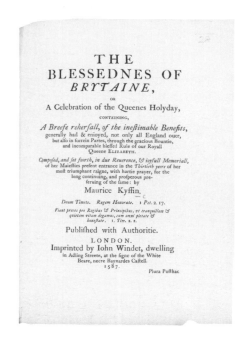

11. Title-page of *The Blessedness of Brytaine*

12. John Davies, poet and "writing school master", of Hereford

an especial emphasis on Gwent, lauds Welshmen in a way which can only be explained by friendships made in the Continental wars. Dedicated to Queen Elizabeth and not without its own incursions into the history of Wales, it is nevertheless both topographical and commendatory of persons far from the Court (including, occasionally, the commonalty).

The accession of the Stuart dynasty in 1603 obviously placed such a euphoria of unity, limited as it may have been to successful Welshmen, under greater strain. The lynchpin of loyalty to a *Welsh* monarch had dropped out. Nevertheless we find the bilingual and prolix John Davies of Hereford (only four miles from the Welsh-speaking lands of Ergyng, it must be remembered) continuing the same grandiloquent tone as his predecessors had used. Addressing the new Prince of Wales, James I's son Henry, in his poem 'Cambria' (1603), he not merely confirms the senior role of Wales in the kingdom of Britain but reveals, interestingly, his consciousness of the interpretative role accorded to the Welshman writing in English. It was his business to explain Wales to the newcomers from Scotland.

> I speake for those, whose Tongues are strange to thee,
> In thine own Tongue; if my words be unfit,
> That blame be mine; but if Wales better be
> By my disgrace, I hold that grace to me.

There is a hint there of his true priorities, which perhaps only the death of Queen Elizabeth could have made plain to him.

The seventeenth century, then, was bound to see changes in the attitudes, if not the origins, of Anglo-Welsh poets. Hugh Holland of Denbigh, European traveller and disappointed courtier, wrote, in his *Pancharis* (1603), probably the most anti-English poem of the century, and the succession to St. Donats of the Sir John Stradling who

13. St. Donat's Castle, home of the Stradling family

founded Cowbridge Grammar School and wrote *Beati Pacifici: a divine poem* (1623) and *Divine Poems* (1625) marks in literary history the erratic but continuing anglicisation of the Welsh gentry. Whereas Sir Edward of the same name, the poet's predecessor and kinsman, had paid for the publication of Sion Dafydd Rhys's *Welsh Grammar* in 1592 and was described (long after his death) by Thomas Wiliems of Trefriw in the Preface to *His Welsh Grammar* as "the chief cherisher of our Welsh language in South Wales", the author of *Beati Pacifici* was born in Bristol and, adopted by the childless Sir John, came to St. Donats after an Oxford education and travels on the continent. The breach in the line here was responsible for the change of language, but elsewhere English ate into the top of the social rampart with a greater inevitability. That the process should not be telescoped by heedless generalisation, however, is demonstrated by an instance from the eighteenth and nineteenth centuries, when two changes of locality and three generations created Sir Lewis Morris, the Anglo-Welsh poet, out of the direct line from Lewis Morris (*Llewelyn Ddu o Fôn*), one of the three Morris brothers who between them revitalised *Welsh* writing at a time of spiritual crisis.

The early confidence of Welshmen writing in English out of a 'favoured' position was bound to disappear, though the political atmosphere was slower to change than one might expect. The English poems of Richard Wiliam (*Syr Risiart y Fwyalchen*), written some time between 1590 and 1630, do little more than indicate the increasing bilingualism of the Vale of Glamorgan. William Harbert's *A Prophesie of Cadwallader, Last King of the Britaines* (1604) is a continuation, in content and attitude, of the writing of Kyffin and Davies. James I pandered to Welshmen about the Court (such as the Earl of Worcester and Sir Philip Herbert, his Secretary of State) with talk of a 'pan-Celtic alliance', and it was only gradually that – despite the eminence of John Williams, Dean of Westminster and Keeper of the Great Seal, and the interest of Ben Jonson, who learned Welsh and wrote a masque entitled 'For the Honour of Wales' in 1619 – it could be noticed that those Court Welshmen were greatly diminished in number. The universities, indeed, began to supplant the Court as the main source of verse in English. David Lloyd of Llanidloes's picaresque and braggart *The Legend of Captain Jones* (1631) may seem a strange poem from a cleric: it is perhaps not less important that it came out of the seclusion of All Souls. And William Vaughan of Golden Grove, whose *The Church Militant* (1640) is rightly thought a tedious work, could write, as though from Newfoundland, a much livelier doggerel battle called *The Golden Fleece* (1626), in which St. David defends the honour of Wales against the 'Dogrel Rimers' Scogin and Skelton. Lloyd, Harbert and Vaughan, be it noted, were all Oxford men.

So, of course, was Henry Vaughan, by far the most significant poet to be mentioned thus far. Born at Newton-by-Scethrog in the Usk valley in 1621, he learned Welsh at his mother's knee but does not appear, in his maturity, to have had any real knowledge of writing in that language, or indeed of its poetic tradition. The stance he adopted in his poetry (apropos his native land) was the interpretative one first noticed in John Davies of Hereford and the reasons for this lie not merely in his education but in his earliest poetic contacts. While in London Vaughan seems to have belonged to a literary circle which included the youthful Katherine Fowler (later to marry James Philipps of Cardigan and achieve poetic renown as 'the matchless Orinda') and his neighbour John Jeffreys of Abercynrig in the Usk valley: his mentor, both at home and at Oxford,

14. 'The Matchless Orinda' (Mrs. Katherine
Philipps) by Farthorne

was Thomas Powell of Cantref, cleric and author of several books and an unpublished
manuscript about the Druids: and his two marriages, to the Wise sisters of Coleshill,
Warwickshire, are the *entré* to a question never yet considered – namely, the focal
power and influence of the household of Sir Herbert Price at The Priory, Brecon,
through which these Midland contacts were sustained. What little emerges in
document about a life that is largely hidden suggests in Henry Vaughan a wide and
curious reading, the driving interests of which were medicine and theology, and early
influences from the Royalist poet and dramatist, William Cartwright. Grief for a
younger brother's death may have been the final impulse to a spiritual conversion
which conditioned the poetry of his maturity. There was also an earlier patriotic desire
(emphasised by his use of the sobriquet 'Silurist') to demonstrate to his erstwhile
companions of Oxford and London days, as well as his Midland in-laws, that his native
Breconshire scene was not merely civilised but could rival, in literary mode, the
classical landscapes of the past. Of this last intention we may learn from his poem 'To
the River Isca':

> *Poets* (like *Angels*) where they once appear
> *Hallow* the *place*, and each succeeding year
> Adds *rev'rence* to't, such as at length doth give
> This aged faith, *That there their Genii live.*

There is no recognition here of Welsh bards gone before: the poet himself will make
Isca celebrated, will make a first mark for his native valley on the topographical record
of the inherited classical scene in English. The love of his native region is not in doubt,
but the Welshness is in the location of it, not in the poetry, which mediates between it
and the audience-in-the mind entirely within the English tradition.

15. Engraved title-page of Henry Vaughan's *Olor Iscanus* (The Swan of Usk), 1651

Henry Vaughan, of course, is not to be netted, in terms of his achievement as a poet, by being placed in this particular Anglo-Welsh succession. Chiefly famed, perhaps, for his devotional collection, *Silex Scintillans* (1650 and 1655), he exceeds the bounds of this – both earlier, in *Poems* (1646) and *Olor Iscanus* (dated December 1647 but not published till 1651), and, later, in *Thalia Rediviva* (1678) – and is a more various poet than his metaphysical reputation suggests. Occasionally incapable of sustaining or matching the magnificent images with which some of his poems begin, he has also been blamed, by critics unaware of the customs of the time, for borrowing from George Herbert (a distant cousin of his, who but for his birth outside Wales – probably either at Eyton, Salop, or London – and the exclusiveness of his poetic attention to the religious life, in the context of his cure at Bemerton, would certainly have been included in the Anglo-Welsh succession). But precisely because Vaughan sometimes seems short of breath poetically he excels from time to time at the building up of brief images, dismissed as soon as drawn, after the fashion of the Welsh practice of *dyfalu* – a practice which has been the basis of an argument for his close acquaintance with the poetic tradition in Welsh. If doubts are cast on this here, it need not diminish our admiration for a stanza such as this from 'Sondayes':

> The pulleys unto headlong man; Time's bower;
> The narrow way;
> Transplanted Paradise; God's walking houre,
> The cool o'th day!
> The creature's jubile; God's parle with dust;
> Heaven here; man on those hills of myrrh, and flowres;
> Angels descending; the returns of trust;
> A gleam of glory, after six-days-showres!

The achievement, not widely recognised until the nineteenth century, is considerable. Henry Vaughan is one of the great 'metaphysicals'.

The valley of the Usk around Llansantffraid was in or near his time not merely the birthplace of such various figures as William Aubrey, 'the great civilian' (1529-95), Leander Jones (1575-1636), the President-General of the English Benedictines who came from Rome in 1634 to offer Archbishop Laud a cardinal's hat, and Jenkin Jones (1623- ?), the Puritan preacher-captain who 'approved' Breconshire for the Parliament: it also harboured the nucleus of a social group with Anglo-Welsh interests (not, as might be suspected, drawn from Puritan infiltrators, but resident, with an Oxford-Royalist-Church of England base) – something which is not detected again as clearly until the nineteenth century. The focus of this has already been mentioned: Sir Herbert Price of The Priory, Brecon, was a great-grandson to the Sir John who in 1534 had defended Geoffrey of Monmouth's *History* against Polydore Vergil's attack and had charged his son to publish his fuller answer under the title of *Historiae Britannicae Defensio* (1573): his wife Goditha was related to the Sir John Denham who wrote 'Cooper's Hill'. This household attracted another poet rather less local and not, as far as is known, Oxford-educated, for whom Sir Herbert was "a walking Library". Rowland Watkyns, who published *Flamma sine Fumo* (1662), was a native of Longtown, on the Herefordshire side of the Black Mountains. He affected to dislike the natives of Breconshire, though his poems (especially after his ejection from his benefice of Llanfrynach) named almost as many of the local gentry as can be found in any single manuscript record. Down-to-earth popularisations of his sermon-themes,

16. Brecknock Priory, 1793, by Sir Richard Colt Hoare

many of them, or portraits with a moral, these poems nevertheless often possess an epigrammatic quality which makes them memorable. 'The new illiterate Lay-Teachers', for instance, is briefly forceful:

> If this a propagation shall be found,
> These build the house, which pull it to the ground;
> This is meere Hocus-Pocus; a strange sight,
> By putting candles out, to gain more light.

IV Exiles, Evangelists and Antiquaries

It is possible, more generally, to distinguish in the seventeenth century two other kinds of writing in English that take their beginning from Wales. The first is one produced by Welshmen long resident in London. Amongst publications of this type may be mentioned *Poetical Piety* (1677), the Preface to which mentions that its author, William Williams, was born near Gogerddan in Cardiganshire. Much more important, and sounding still that horn of pride in Wales which Kyffin and Davies first blew (always a horn best carried by those successful at Court), was the work of James Howell of Abernant, Carmarthenshire. Graduate and non-resident Fellow of Jesus College, Oxford, polyglot businessman, traveller and Royalist secret agent, Howell compiled an English-French-Italian-Spanish dictionary (*Lexicon Tetraglotton*, 1659-60), with an appendix of proverbs from those languages and some from the Welsh, and wrote two long political poems – *Dodona's Grove* (1641), which he signed 'Cambro-Britannus', and *England's Teares* (1644). But his *Familiar Letters (Epistolae Ho-Elianae)*, in four books, published in 1645, constitute his main claim to remembrance. If their rather trivial Royalism is occasionally irritating, at least they offer an entry to a Caroline view of Europe and a wide-ranging parade of contemporary information. Howell may perhaps be described as the first of the 'quality' journalists. More interesting from a Welsh point of view, however, is his *Parly of Beasts, or Morphandra, Queen of the Inexhausted Island* (1660), a prose work in which Orosian talking goat (that is, the Welsh goat) declares that he lives in "the healthfullest country on earth", though the English, who have forgotten that it was the Welsh who introduced them to Christianity, do nothing but twit his countrymen "ever and anon with Leeks and Cheese". The adjective 'inexhausted' may well be applied here to that Welsh pride in 'the Island': the gibes are thrown back where they came from, as Shakespeare threw them back in his portrait of Fluellen. But it should be remembered that Howell was already established commercially in London by 1616, before Ben Jonson wrote his

17. James Howell, traveller, business agent, writer and Royalist spy

masque 'For the Honour of Wales'. There were not many Welshmen to achieve prominence as the century wore on.

The second category of writing had a cause and an origin very different. Puritan in genesis and evangelistic in intention, it was, so to speak, forced to leave Welsh for English because of the overwhelmingly *English* stimulus to the Puritan cause in the seventeenth century and the monoglot English character of the congregations of the faithful. The pull of potential audience was usually complemented by the nature of the poet's experience. Morgan Llwyd (1619-59), a Welsh-speaker from Maentwrog, had early been drawn into Puritan circles in Radnorshire and when, after experience in the Parliamentary army in England, he returned to minister to an Independent congregation in Wrexham, he could not but be aware of the already heavily anglicised nature both of the town and more particularly of the people he ministered to. Of the fifty-two poems in *Gweithiau Morgan Llwyd* thirty-one are in English and occasionally poems in one language are infiltrated by lines and phrases from the other. If English was a second language to Llwyd and his command of stanza-structures in its poetry limited, at least his polemic embodies some of the force of his passion and commitment. The image of 'The Winter' carries through these two stanzas –

> our british climate was so cold, soules frozen were to death
> we were for want of light & zeale a barren tedious heath

> Our northeast cutt to Indies mines, I meane to heavenly gold
> we mist it, summer was so short and winter was so cold

– and is cancelled in a verse from another poem:

> O Wales, poor Rachel, thou shalt beare
>   sad Hannah now rejoyce
> The last is first, the summer comes
>   to heare the turtles voice.

This is a new note in English verse from Wales.

A century later *Hosanna to the Son of David* (1759), the first of William Williams Pantycelyn's two collections of verse in English, had similar considerations of

18. William Williams, Pantycelyn. Engraving by Mackenzie from *Holl Weithiau*, 1867

readership in mind. English-speaking Gower and South Pembrokeshire, on his one hand, Radnorshire and East Breconshire, already unevenly anglicised, on the other, were both of them important fields of Methodist endeavour, which Williams from his home near Llandovery could not ignore – at least until the Welsh Calvinists took their leave of John Wesley. The line stretches on, through *Hymns on Various Subjects* (1771) by Peter Williams of Llansadyrnin, Carmarthenshire, another Methodist preacher and author, prolific in Welsh, for a further two decades.

Methodism in the eighteenth century produced two lay poets, of whom one probably had no language other than English. But the evangelical urge was no less. The first of these was Jane Cave, daughter of a Brecon glover who had originally come from Dorset to Talgarth as an exciseman. Her *Poems on Various Subjects, Entertaining, Elegiac and Religious* (1783) is a collection interesting mainly for its elegies (there is one on 'the death of the Rev. Mr. Howel Harris'): its versifying rarely exceeds the competent, and the poetic impetus, as against the religious, is low. The second poet-layman was Walter Churchey of Brecon, whose Arminian stance enabled him to look direct to John Wesley, who was personally responsible for collecting subscriptions for *Poems and Imitations of the British Poets, with Odes, Miscellanies and Notes*, a volume of 832 pages which appeared in 1789. Wesley's early reluctance to assist was entirely justified by the result: the critics did not bother to read the 226 pages of Churchey's longest poem, 'The Life of Joseph'. Nor were his subsequent books more successful.

With the severe diminution of Wesleyan activity in Wales (after the breach with Whitfield), evangelical writing of the kind described disappeared for a time, only to reappear when the invasion of south-east Wales by English-speaking multitudes enforced a new appraisal of the situation by Welsh poets. *The English Poems* (1913) of *Islwyn* (Rev. William Thomas), thought by many to have been the outstanding poet writing in Welsh in the nineteenth century, were no doubt a reflection of increasing English settlement within reach of his home at Babell in the Rhymney valley, and

19. The Reverend William Thomas: the poet *Islwyn*

Songs in the Night (1885) and *Tristiora* (1896), the technically sophisticated English poems of the Swansea-born Calvinistic Methodist minister John Hughes, most of whose work is in Welsh, again represent an overflow of the Nonconformist spirit into an increasingly bilingual situation. This is demonstrated even more clearly by William Parry's *The Old Evangelist* (1893), the subject of the title-poem of which was William Evans, Calvinistic Methodist minister of Tonyrefail, who had died two years before. Parry added a dedication to John Elias, Christmas Evans and William Williams o'r Wern, the three great men, each from a different denomination, who had dominated preaching in Welsh up to 1840. After these wrestlings with a new situation, the bilingualism of *Elfed* (Howell Elvet Lewis, 1860-1953) appears very relaxed. Born at Cynwyl, Carmarthenshire, and for long minister at King's Cross Tabernacl in London, he had a natural linguistic gift which gives some of his hymns in English (of which 'Lamb of God, unblemished' and 'Whom oceans part, O Lord, unite' are perhaps the best known) a quality comparable with the best.

To do no more than indicate a line of succession through such 'sports' of an essentially Welsh Dissent, however, is to obscure what had really happened in Wales between the time of Morgan Llwyd and that of Pantycelyn. Briefly, the pride and confidence of successful Welshmen at the time of the Union had almost totally collapsed by the end of the seventeenth century, and early Dissent did little to restore it because it was of English origin, affecting only the English-speaking and bilingual districts of Flintshire, Denbighshire, Radnorshire and eastern Gwent. It was not until the Circulating Schools of Gruffydd Jones, together with the preaching of Howel Harris and Daniel Rowland (and the breach with John Wesley), had made mid-eighteenth century Methodism *Welsh* that a new Wales was created – ignorant, maybe, of all else but the Bible, but capable of retaining its own values and unaffected by the snobberies beyond its borders. It is plain that there was not, and could not be, any verse in English, other than the evangelical surplus already described, which took its origin from this separate Welsh 'world'.

An older Welsh tradition, however, antiquarian and eisteddfodic in character, was more prolific of writing in English. The poets in this were Welsh-speaking and in most cases the burden of their work was in Welsh, but they, too, were affected, and rather earlier, by the pressures towards English. One of the factors involved was the presence of some of them in London, where the interpretative role seemed more imperative. And this role was supported by the prevailing outlook of metropolitan Societies like the Cymmrodorion, the Gwyneddigion and the Caradogion, whose members adopted towards the Welsh antiquities which they worked to preserve an attitude which was defensively sentimental rather than vindicatory. There were, as with *Iolo Morganwg*, moments of defiance, but the prevailing tone, not unconnected with a Churchmanship conscious of the hostility of its own hierarchy, was explicatory: it asked, at best, that the Welsh heritage should be regarded as 'curious' and 'different': if it still dreamed of Tudor assertions of pride and seniority in the history of the island of Britain it did not dare to speak of them.

The case of those in Wales was a little more various. Of Lewis Morris of Llanfihangel Tre'r-beirdd, Anglesey (1701-65), it must be sufficient to say that he was the greatest mid-eighteenth century authority on the Welsh language and that his few poems in English, like 'The Fishing Lass of Hakin', are the result of an overflow of ebullience into another language with which he was perfectly familiar from his work as Deputy-

20. Lewis Morris: *Llewelyn Ddu o Fôn*

Steward of the Crown manors in Cardiganshire. Possibly, too, he accepted the interpretative role both in his instigation, through his brother Richard, of the foundation of the Cymmrodorion Society in 1751 and in his preparation of prose works in English, particularly his dictionary of Welsh place-names, entitled *Celtic Remains*, which he intended to have published by that Society. *Ieuan Brydydd Hir* or *Ieuan Fardd* (Evan Evans of Lledrod, 1731-88), differed most of all in being less fortunate. A disciple of Lewis Morris, he in turn became the greatest Welsh scholar of his age, and his many curacies and total lack of preferment in the Church of England emphasised that institution's contemporary anti-Welsh bias. 'The Love of our Country' (1772), his only poem in English, was probably a response to the help he received from English-speaking sympathisers like Sir Watkin Williams Wynn II, Paul Panton and Thomas Pennant.

David Samwell (*Dafydd Ddu Feddyg*, 1751-98) was a much-travelled naval surgeon resident in London in his later years. 'The Padouca Hunt' (1791) and 'The Negro Boy' (not published till 1798) were the result of controversies in which members of the London Welsh Societies engaged – that surrounding the Welsh Indians, in the first case, and, in the other, the wider, humanitarian one about slavery. For *Iolo Morganwg*, born Edward Williams at Llancarfan in the Vale of Glamorgan, the issues were more complex. English was the tongue he learned at his mother's knee, and though his life was devoted to ancient literature in Welsh (some of which he took care to create himself), he was familiar with the modish English poetry of his time, particularly that of Shenstone and Collins. One of his motives in writing extensively in English – his *Poems Lyric and Pastoral* (1794) runs to two volumes and over 400 pages – was undoubtedly a desire to show that a country stonemason was a match for the best of his English contemporaries: another was equally certainly a patriotism which became increasingly vituperative. It is a pity, then, that what he wrote in English so rarely escapes the merely competent and imitative. His 'Address to the Inhabitants of Wales, exhorting them to emigrate with William Penn, to Pennsylvania', which he purported to have translated from the Welsh of an anonymous emigrant, reflects his interest in

21. *Iolo Morganwg* (Edward Williams),
stonemason, poet and creator of the Gorsedd

Madoc and the story of the Welsh Indians. "Tyranny", he writes, "with shameless face / Enslaves your native plains" – there is only one course open:

> Boast, CAMBRIA, boast thy sceptred Lord, —
> 'Twas HE, thy Madoc, first explored
> What bounds th' Atlantic tide;
> He, from the tumults of a Crown,
> Sought shelter in a *world unknown*,
> With HEAV'N his only guide.

The sentiments apart, it is not a language with the life and energy that a Welsh foray into English demands.

The line of succession from *Iolo* is direct, for the next poet in the eisteddfodic tradition who concerns us here was Taliesin Williams (1787-1847), none other than his son. A schoolmaster at Merthyr Tydfil, an antiquary and a prominent *eisteddfodwr*, Taliesin wrote two long poems in English – *Cardiff Castle* (1827) and *The Doom of Colyn Dolphyn* (1837) – both of which, liberally supplied with historical notes, were attempts to preach a local patriotism to an increasingly bilingual readership in Glamorgan. The verse is always subservient to the history, which has been described as "comparatively worthless", but the structural control of the verse and the occasional unexpected but happily placed word render the writing of Taliesin Williams in English comparable with, if not superior to, that of his father. *The Doom of Colyn Dolphyn* has considerable narrative impetus.

Cambria upon Two Sticks (1867) is the more varied work of John Thomas (*Ieuan Ddu*, 1795-1871). Thomas again was a schoolmaster at Merthyr (as well as at Machen, Pontypridd and Treforest) and could not but be aware that the English in which he taught was making rapid progress amongst the young. Known to posterity chiefly as musician, *eisteddfodwr*, and writer on musical subjects, he seems to have regarded his English verse as a useful vent for satire. Canto I of 'Cambria upon Two Sticks' begins:

> Ye English prigs who drive our Welsh prigs mad
> By scouting rites that made our fathers glad . . .

and later proceeds:

> 'Tween party wranglers I'll once dare, though loth,
> Their prejudice to bare in sight of both . . .

A long poem in two cantos in the same volume, entitled 'Harry Vaughan', is ostensibly about a 'young gentleman', deprived of Welsh by his social status, who encounters two bulls and two young ladies by the mouth of the Tywi. All its interest, however, is in its digressions: its dual purpose is to laud the poet's native place, Carmarthen, and to indicate his breadth of reading in the English poets and his lack of reverence for some of them. Occasionally his asides are very apt. Of the Edward Young of 'Night Thoughts' he writes:

> Young too is great, so very great indeed,
> That oft we wish he knew how to be less;
> Or, that his soul from big thoughts were so free'd
> As not to make his song seem his distress.

And of his regard for the Welsh language there can be no doubt:

> Some say, the Welsh doth nurse our native vices,
>   And cause rebellion, riots and what not?
> And oft the landlord whose small farm's high price is
>   So shameful, knows of Welsh, no, not one jot?
> If Welshmen have a fault, 'tis that their slices
>   Of their right's loaf to a mere crumb is brought;
> And but infers at last, the English tongue
> Alone can save our skins from English wrong.

This is not gifted work, either in punctuation or language. But *Ieuan Ddu* is rarely less than combative and his escape from the stereotypes of writing so far noted makes his work more stimulating than that of most of his nineteenth century Anglo-Welsh contemporaries.

It cannot be without significance that the Eisteddfod itself was responsible for the appearance of a limited quantity of verse in English. John Lloyd, for instance, the Breconshire poet of whom more will be said presently, won the prize at the Cardiff Eisteddfod of 1834 with his 'Ode to the Princess Victoria'. S.C. Gamwell of Swansea was adjudged by Lewis Morris and *Dewi Môn* to have written a poem on 'Brecknock Castle' worthy of the prize at the Brecon Eisteddfod of 1889. William Williams of Pontypool proudly proclaimed himself 'Chaired Bard' on the title-page and cover of his *Songs of Siluria* (1916), quoting nine poems as chair-winning and another seventeen as 'prize poems'. Lloyd, Gamwell, Williams and others create a new eisteddfodic category, for it is unlikely that any of them spoke or wrote Welsh. The resulting poems, however – with titles chosen from a suitably distant history (like 'The Massacre of Seisyllt ap Dyfnal in Abergavenny Castle') – were uniformly undistinguished. The best that could have been said for competitions of this kind was that they associated a limited number of English-speakers, sentimentally and without contemporary overtones, with the historical vicissitudes of Wales.

The collective impression made by the works of another class of bilingual writers, the clergy of the Church of England, improves on this scarcely at all. To write in English was for some of them – like David Hughes (*fl.* 1770-1817), the parsonical headmaster of Ruthin School – not much more than a reflection of their belief that their status demanded it and that the Welsh language was heading for extinction. Others, like Thomas Marsden, whose collection *The Poet's Orchard* appeared in 1848, were attempting to use verse for the same evangelical purpose as the Methodists had done. Eliezer Williams (Peter Williams's son), whose *Nautical Odes, or poetical sketches, designed to commemorate the achievements of the British Navy* (1801) indicated that, after service in England and as a naval chaplain, he had settled for a wider British Patriotism, and Edward 'Celtic' Davies, whose *Aphtharte, the Genius of Britain* was published in 1784, were among the more noteworthy of the remainder. Davies, his patriotism sharpened by exile, was deeply interested not merely in the Druids but in the poetry of the *Cynfeirdd* and the *Gogynfeirdd* and his long poem 'Chepstow' demonstrates some of the theories about landscape initiated by William Gilpin in his *Observations on the River Wye* (1782). Francis Homfray's *Thoughts on Happiness* (he is described as 'Rector of Lanvayer Kilgeddine') had achieved a second edition from a London publisher by 1817, and John Jones (*Joannes Towy*), who published *Newport Castle and Other Short Poems* 1886, threw no little light, by means of his descriptions and dedications, on the Pembrokeshire of his life and times.

None of these, however, except possibly Marsden, whose anti-Catholicism obsessed him, made any adequate response to the spiritual, political or social conditions in which their lives were lived. It is the unease and bitterness of *Goronva Camlann* (Rowland Williams 1817-70), whose *Lays from the Cimbric Lyre* appeared in 1846, which marks him out for longer scrutiny. A Classics don at Cambridge whose childhood and youth were spent at Meifod, he was a Churchman of modernist views and a patriot prepared to argue the permanent value of the teaching of Welsh. The patriotic note he sounded, it is true, was often safely relegated to the long ago, but the bitterness is unmistakable:

> With open hand the Saxon came,
> And lured us with his daughter's smile —
> What knew we of the smouldering flame?
> Woe, woe the time.

That is the opening stanza of 'The Banquet of Salisbury Plain', with which his book begins. Almost alone from his century, he answers the pride of Kyffin, John Davies of Hereford and James Howell with the realisation of disappointment, of history gone awry. 'To the Prince of Wales' begins like this:

> How can I pay the homage of the heart,
>   When thou art scarce of British race?
> How can I play the courtier's busie part,
>   Or robe in smiles my eager face?
> Scarcelie a lingering drop of Tudor blood
>   In all thy veins retains its force;
> Yet dearer far to me, than all the flood
>   From Gothic and polluted source.

Present personally at the Prince's baptism at Windsor, he goes on to show himself partly mollified by the occasion, but his reasons for using a pseudonym are apparent enough: his appointment in 1850 as Vice-Principal of St. David's College, Lampeter, could hardly have happened if he had been identified beforehand by his espousal of a separate Welsh tradition and his attacks on the subservient Englishness of his Church.

V The First Anglo-Welsh: The Gentry

Another category of male poets from within Wales, some of whom were bilingual – namely, those who were neither evangelical nor clerical nor antiquarian nor eisteddfodic – is more varied both in character and quality. One or two of them, of course, blur the artificial boundaries created.

Richard Llwyd of Beaumaris (1752-1835), although deeply interested in Welsh antiquities, was nevertheless influenced most by his father's life in the coastal trade and his own stewardship to one of the gentry. When he came to write, his local patriotism, as expressed in his best-known work, *Beaumaris Bay* (1800), found its outlet in English. Thomas Jeffery Llewelyn Prichard (1790-1862), born plain Thomas Prichard at Builth, began to show his enthusiasm for Welsh antiquities while in London (where he had presumably been an actor for some years) by contributing to the early issues of *The Cambro-Briton* during the editorship of John Humffreys Parry (1819-22). Back in Wales in 1824, he published *Welsh Minstrelsy*, containing 'The Land Beneath the Sea or Cantrev y Gwaelod', a poem which made Tennyson laugh when he read it at Aberystwyth in 1839. Canto I begins:

> And art thou lost beneath the waters —
> Once loveliest of Cymru's daughters! —
> Thou flosculous and fruitful fair one!
> The sun has wept his perish'd rare one,
> As weeps the heart-rent widow'd lover
> His chosen maid whose smiles are over...

If the word 'flosculous' does indeed invite laughter, this passage nevertheless demonstrates a rhythmic liveliness which appears again in poems like 'The Sevi-Lan-Gwy'. In such a substantial volume (of 273 pages) there are many dull and unremarkable pieces, but a few, like 'My Lowly Love', fitly match the energy with which Prichard personally enrolled the 811 subscribers to his volume.

Rustiness in Welsh as well as long residence in London no doubt determined Prichard's choice of language for his writing. A comparable, but final, absence from Wales affected John Jones ('Poet Jones' to his Stalybridge neighbours). Born at

22. Richard Llwyd, 'The Bard of Snowdon'.
Portrait by W. Jones of Chester

Llanasa, Flintshire, in 1788, he served in the Navy and afterwards worked in a Lancashire mill. *Poems by John Jones* (1856) was a small volume intended, inevitably, for an English readership. In the case of Titus Lewis (1822-87) from Llanelly, a life in trade was that factor which dominated choice. A representative for a firm of Manchester warehousemen, he came to live at Llanblethian in the Vale of Glamorgan (itself an increasingly anglicised area): and although he became noted as an antiquary, his verse in English – particularly his lengthy work, *The Soldier's Wife, a Tale of Inkerman* (1855) – reflects both a knowledge of a wider world and that pride of participation in empire (already seen in Eliezer Williams) which was several steps further along the road to 'acceptance' than any of the attitudes noted amongst the Cymmrodorion figures at the turn of the previous century. He was writing, after all, in the age of Victoria.

The one remaining poet in the category discussed had an outlook politically rather than theologically radical. Thomas Jenkins (1774-1843), the youngest son of the vicar of Meidrim and Brechfa, acted towards the end of his life as clerk to the Carmarthen solicitor Hugh Williams, now believed to have been the orchestrator of the Rebecca Riots. His intellectual life (like that of many another from the counties of Carmarthen and Cardigan and, most notably, like that of the Morris brothers of Anglesey) was conducted in English – a feature again of the *Diary* of his artisan son Thomas (published for the first time in 1975). The *Miscellaneous Poems* (1845) of Thomas Jenkins senior were a posthumous collection, published by his niece Ann Matilda Waugh, wife of the vicar of Llanvetherine, who herself had published a volume of verse entitled *The Wreath of Gwent*. Radical poems there are in Jenkins's collection, but they are well bolstered by ballads and lyrical trivia. He can be as sententious as any contemporary —

> In my earliest days, ere sorrows had ever
> > Been known, e'en to fancy, or once caused a thought;
> Delighted I strayed in the shades of DYNEVOR,
> > Enjoying its beauties and pleasures unbought

— but in general his lines are tauter and more rhythmic than those of most of his rivals.

Amongst those versifiers whose only language was English the gentry, of course, were prominent. What is surprising, in view of John Wesley's comment upon the *number* of gentry in Pembrokeshire, is that that county did not produce proportionately more of them. Roger Lort of Stackpole (1608-64) has been quoted as one of the few, but his only book of poems, *Epigrammatum Liber Primus* (1646), was in Latin. George Stepney (1663-1707), though certainly descended from the Prendergast family of that name, spent all his life in London, Cambridge or on the Continent and never, as far as is known, evinced enough interest in Wales either to visit it or write about it. Sir John Scourfield, born Philipps in 1808, is therefore the first from *Anglia Transwallina* who may reasonably be counted. Born at Williamston on the Cleddau, he was educated at Harrow and Oxford, was a Member of Parliament for twenty-four years, and published a number of books of poems, of which the second was punningly entitled *Lyrics and Philippics* (1859). His first venture (*c.* 1847) had been a skit on the newly founded and intentionally Welsh College at Llandovery and a number of his later poems concern themselves with Wales in the mode the writer's class and interest would lead one to expect.

23. Sir Charles Hanbury-Williams, satirist
and diplomat. Portrait by R. Rhodes,
after Mengs, 1820

The career of Sir Charles Hanbury-Williams (1708-59) – one of the industrialist family of Hanbury of Pontypool, who were entirely English in blood (the Williams being appended by Sir Charles, a fourth son, on the receipt of a legacy from a friend of his father's) – is inevitably a corrective to generalisation. Established at Coldbrook House in Monmouthshire, he entered Parliament as the Member for Gloucester, became Paymaster of Marine, insatiable beau and lover of Peg Woffington. Tiring of this life after fourteen years, he was appointed Ambassador first to Saxony and subsequently to Russia, where his initial success depended upon his close relationship with the future Catherine the Great. His poetical works, which were published in three volumes in 1822, consist largely of political lampoons, very much in vogue during Walpole's ascendancy.

Far more staid, though surprising in a different way, is the little volume entitled *The Horrors of Invasion* by Robert Holland Price of Llangollen, a second edition of which was printed in 1804. In this minuscule 'long poem' the author, regretting his own ill-health, calls on the Welsh – and exclusively, citing Aneirin, Llywarch Hen and Owain Cyfeiliog as his precedents – to resist the aggression of Bonaparte –

> Shew them the gen'rous stock from whence you spring,
> Defend your country, guard your pious king!

– picturing each of the officers of the Chirk Hundred Volunteers, whom he names, in heroic stance fronting the enemy. The combination here of reference to a far Welsh past, rather than to the kingly glories of the Tudors, with an unquestioning acceptance of the 'union' of Britain in the present, is unusual in any writer of the time, and even more so in one who calls himself so determinedly 'Gent'.

George Powell of Nanteos (1842-82), though initially a misfit in a gentlemanly background, in the end proved true to Eton, Oxford and comparative wealth. Guilty of versifying a good deal (and weakly) before he was twenty, under the pseudonym of *Miölnir Nanteos*, he became in later years a dilettante, a collector of books and music, a close friend of Swinburne and an admirer of Wagner. His main achievement lay in the

24. Nanteos, later the home of George Powell. Drawing by Sir Samuel Rush Meyrick

translation, with Eiríkr Magnusson, of Icelandic legends (published in 1864 and 1866), and his chief talent was for music. Though he was generous locally when he came to be master of Nanteos, for such short time as he had, he had nothing to say to or about Wales.

John Lloyd of Dinas, Brecon (1797-1875), though likewise educated at Eton and Oxford, was made of rather different stuff. His *Poems*, published in 1847 and reprinted in the year of his death, were encouraged by his success at the National Eisteddfod at Cardiff in 1834. In them he reveals, surprisingly, Parliamentarian sympathies in a number of poems about the Civil War (he had a great admiration for Hampden) and calls not infrequently on Llywelyn, Glyndŵr and other Welsh heroes in verse that, unfortunately, shows no more than a modest talent. Lloyd writes copiously about the Breconshire scene, which was obviously dear to him, and reveals a reservation or two about the imperial enthusiasms of his time. The opening lines from his poem 'On the River Usk' reveal the curious limbo in which Henry Vaughan's reputation lay until Alexander Grosart republished his work in 1871:

> Usk, tho' unknown to song thou may not vie
> With the famed windings of the sylvan Wye,
> With Towy glorying in her Grongar's shade,
> Or Avon sacred by a Shakespeare made;
> Yet art thou dearer far, for on thy side
> From boyhood have I stray'd, and seen thee glide
> Like a companion when none else was near
> Whisp'ring thine own sweet language on mine ear . . .

VI The First Anglo-Welsh: The Bourgeoisie

Plainly the gentry were not in every case prisoners of their caste, even if education and upbringing necessarily confined them to English. Nor, of course, were English monoglots of lower estate. What is noticeable about the latter is that they belong to the small towns of the recently anglicised areas of Wales – not to Gower or South Pembrokeshire but to Breconshire and Montgomeryshire.

The earliest to appear was George Thomas. Born about 1791 in Newtown into the woolstapling business, he spent his mature life at Llandyssil in the same county, where in his last years he was both schoolmaster and postmaster. In 1817 he published *The Otter Hunt and the Death of Roman*, a doggerel descriptive work, intended for public recitation, in which the emphasis lies on the misadventures of the inebriated participants. Montgomeryshire, which within a few decades was to produce the prose writing of Nimrod and in the twentieth century that of Geraint Goodwin, deserves special notice not merely as Wales's only region of black-and-white houses but as the home of rural sports so widely popular as to transcend some of the notions of class. But Thomas was to move on to writing more political. After a rather dull poem called *The Welsh Flannel*, whose main purpose seems to have been to celebrate Newtown as the Leeds of Wales, he revealed his firmly Tory stance in *History of the Chartists and the Bloodless Wars of Montgomeryshire* (1840), a poem in five loosely connected parts, which variously satirise the local Yeomanry and their Chartist opponents. Like Robert Holland Price, he names or appears to name individuals among the Yeomanry, but his intention is caricature after the style of Samuel Butler's *Hudibras* (which in turn, interestingly enough, was influenced by the burlesque manner of *The Legend of Captain Jones* by David Lloyd, Montgomeryshire's earliest poet). Thomas's most outrageous character is the monstrous Sergeant Webb, coward, glutton and snobbish *poseur*:

> Hur keen as crow gunpowder smelt,
> And did not wish to risk hur pelt,
> Hur wass ass Welsh attorney big,
> And wore a carrot-colour'd wig,
> For plague call'd scab make Welsh sheep bare
> And other plagues rot Welshmen's hair,
> Hur came from place call'd *Mawr Cern'og*,
> And call'd hur *Ceffel Yscy farnog*,
> Hur vow'd ere hur was take lead pill,
> Hur'd with good things hur belly fill,
> And then sit down to make hur will.

This is verse, undoubtedly, in which the literary element is meekly subservient to contemporary appeal. But it has more life than the work of Newtown's other mid-nineteenth century poet, George Baxter. Born at Llanllwchaiarn (which is Newtown-across-the-bridge) in 1815, Baxter was distantly descended from the Shropshire divine of that surname, but his family had long been resident in English-speaking Montgomeryshire. His publications, *Don Juan Junior: A Poem by Byron's Ghost* (1839) and *A History of the Working of the Poor Law* (1841), reflect interests that were more widely intellectual but not for that reason livelier.

25. A View of Brecon, by J.M. Ince, 1850

The next three poets to be mentioned were all denizens of Brecon town. Richard Hall (1817-66) was a dispensing chemist who lies buried in Llanspyddid churchyard. Little more of him is known than that, though he seems to have been a native of Brecon and had a shop in Ship Street, he published in 1850 *A Tale of the Past, and Other Poems*. Although a townsman, Hall was devoted to rural pursuits and these lines from 'Fenny Fach Revisited' offer some of the flavour both of his enthusiasms and of the tauter and more interesting verse of which he was capable:

> When hoar-frosts first with dazzling beauty creep,
> Crisping the earth, and making clear the deep,
> Where rolls the river monarch in his pride,
> The poacher's eye soon spies his gleaming side;
> The grappling hooks are with precision thrown,
> Fixed with a jerk – the fated fish dives down
> The pool's dark depths, then, darting out the tide
> Tears forth the keen barbs from its wounded side,
> And seeks in watery caves a hiding lair . . .

The author of *Isolda, or The Maid of Kidwelly and Other Poems* (1851) calls himself on his title-page 'D.Rice Jones Aberhonddu'. But in every other respect he is a shadowy figure. His poem 'The Priory Grove' (which is a long way after Vaughan), makes it plain that he was in Brecon as a boy, and the Preface asks the reader to excuse "the effusions of a young Welsh mountaineer". The shorter pieces in the book, mostly written "at a very early age", are many of them addressed to Laura, Sylvia, Mary and other poet-patronised ladies, and it was probably the long poem 'Isolda' which achieved the support of Lady Charlotte Guest, to whom the volume is dedicated. There is a gesture here towards Welsh tradition —

> Sweet Harp of Cambria! I would fain
> Arouse thy slumbering strings again

— but the poem's narrative, gushing with blood as it is, contrives to be both confusing and in every respect undistinguished.

Rhys Davies, the town surveyor of Brecon, wrote mainly in Welsh under the bardic title of *Llew Lywel*. Born at Trecastle in 1844, he published his *Sketches in Wales* in 1876. It is a volume of light-hearted skits and squibs, of the sort one might expect to hear at a *Noson Lawen*, and the few English pieces are described as 'songs', with a well-known tune prescribed. Some of these are very tolerably amusing, although no longer topical. 'John Jones and John Bull', for instance, touches a Welsh nerve:

> But still John Jones fail'd to grow wealthy,
> And of sorrows and troubles was full;
> He sold his old house at Tycwtta
> To a gentleman by name John Bull . . .

— and later in the same poem:

> Firm fortresses of our forefathers,
> Where no bold invader *dare* lurk,
> But Scotty came over from Gowrie,
> Now the lord of our heights is McTurk.

Rhys Davies was Secretary of the National Eisteddfod when it was held in Brecon in 1889 and it is arguable that his work belongs to the category already occupied by *eisteddfodwyr* like Taliesin Williams and John Thomas. But its lack of high seriousness and its devotion to the local scene mark it as the product of a clear linguistic frontier: its author was a man from the Welsh-speaking lands west of Brecon who, through his own education at Christ College and his experience with the many monoglot English-speakers of the town, was only too aware of the need to include the townsmen in the *Welsh* experience. There are almost no signs in the book of English *poetic* models.

Of the last poet in this category and of his work the opposite is undoubtedly true. Clifford King, born Smith in the workhouse at Hay and educated in a Hay school, published *The Royal Pearl and Other Poems* (1894) and at least four other volumes of verse. *New Poems* (1921) runs to three volumes and two thousand pages. King was totally immersed in the rapidly-weakening nineteenth century Romantic tradition and *Times Literary Supplement*, not unjustly, credited him at best with "an immense fecundity of diction". Any hope here of the achievement of a W.H. Davies is nullified by the absence, amongst so many words, of a sufficient poetic personality.

VII Women Writers in the Early Period

It may appear no more than male chauvinism to indicate here a separate category of women poets, but in truth, society before the nineteenth century having been severely restrictive of female initiative, reasons have to be sought (where no unanswerable talent exists) for the emergence of as many as six women – of whom two, Jane Cave and Ann Matilda Waugh, have been mentioned already. And indeed there is one reason which links the remaining four: three of them, though Welsh-born, either went to London and stayed there or found a husband with a metropolitan origin and life-style: the fourth was born in London and returned there from Wales in later life.

The first of the three is Jane Brereton, born Jane Hughes at Bryn Griffith near Mold in 1685. She married the English dramatist Thomas Brereton and began after her husband's death to contribute verse to *The Gentleman's Magazine*. In 1744, after *her* death, her *Poems on Several Occasions* found a publisher in London. Anne Penny, the second, was the daughter of Bulkely Hughes, vicar of Bangor. She became a resident of Bloomsbury Square after her marriage and of her several published works *Poems with a Dramatic Entertainment* (1771) at least earned a reprinting in 1780 (which was also the year of her death). One of her pieces is entitled 'Taliesin's Poem to Elphin', but in general she made little use of Welsh subjects. Anna Williams (1706-83) of Rosemarket, Pembrokeshire – the third of the three – might reasonably have been listed with the Englishry of that county, but the operative factor in her case was her removal with her father to London in 1727, where the wretched circumstances of her later life were mitigated by shelter and assistance from Samuel Johnson. It was with his help that *Miscellanies in Prose and Verse* was published in 1766.

Jane Williams (*Ysgafell*, as she was later known) was born in Chelsea in 1806 but was sent, when quite young, to Neuadd Felen, near Talgarth, for her health's sake. Here she began to acquire a knowledge of Welsh, made the acquaintance of Lady Llanover and began what was to be a long literary career. Her first publication, *Miscellaneous Poems*, was privately printed at Brecon in 1824 (when she was still only eighteen) and amongst many subsequent works *The Literary Remains* of the Rev. Thomas Price, Carnhuanawc (1854-55), *Celtic Fables, Fairy Tales and Legends Versified* (1862) and *A*

26. Anna Williams, poet, of Rosemarket. Portrait from Boswell, The Life of Samuel Johnson, *1863*

27. *'Children Cutting Out Paper People'.*
Watercolour by Lady Llanover for Jane
Williams's The Origin, Rise and Progress
of the Paper People, 1856

History of Wales (to the end of the Tudor period) (1869) are the most significant. The last-mentioned book was not superseded until J.E. Lloyd's work reached fruition in the first decade of the twentieth century and Jane Williams was undoubtedly one of the earliest writers to explore the Welsh heritage in English in considered, if not wholly academic, fashion. She is, however, not likely to be celebrated for her poetry.

VIII Immigrants and English Models

It is a consideration of the feminine contribution to Anglo-Welsh poetry that leads us most immediately into the fundamental difficulty: whether it is right and proper to consider as 'Anglo-Welsh' the work of writers who, though not Welsh by birth or family, lived in Wales for a substantial proportion of their writing lives. In the second half of the twentieth century it may be possible to 'discard' some such writers on the ground that they speak neither to nor about Wales, but in centuries earlier such a criterion is only partly applicable and residence, in a time when people moved their homes much less frequently, should count proportionately more. Three ladies are the first amongst poets to make a stricter shibboleth unpronounceable.

The latest of the three chronologically is the easiest to assimilate. Anne Beale (1816-1900), though not a native of Wales, lived at or near Llandeilo for upwards of forty years. Her *Poems* (1842), the Preface to which is dated from 'Llwynhelig, Llandilo', was merely the first of many volumes, amongst which is to be found *The Vale of Towey, or Sketches in South Wales* (1844). This book was reissued as *Traits and Stories of the Welsh Peasantry* in 1849 and few writers of English origin have dealt so appreciatively with the rural society of Wales.

Julia Ann Hatton, née Kemble (1764-1838), better known as Ann of Swansea, appears to have come to Wales less willingly. A younger sister of Sarah Siddons but born in Worcester, she had embarrassed her family publicly while in London and in 1799, when she and her second husband, William Hatton, returned from New York, they settled in Swansea with an allowance from her brother and sister which was conditional (like the arrangement made when Richard Savage was exiled to Swansea) on their remaining more than 150 miles from London. They first took a lease of The Bathing House but William Hatton died in 1806 and his widow attempted to establish a dancing-school in Kidwelly. It was on her return to Swansea in 1809 that there began a period of intense literary activity. Between that year and her death in 1838 she published a 139-poem volume called *Poetic Trifles*, a play (*Zaffine*) for Edmund Kean, and at least a dozen novels. When she was no more than nineteen she had had

28. 'Ann of Swansea' (Julia Ann Hatton).
Portrait by Henry Watkeys, 1834

29. 'Swansea Bay', engraved from a drawing by A. Wilson. From Thomas Rees, *Beauties of South Wales*

published in London a first book entitled *Poems on Miscellaneous Subjects* and in her long poem 'Swansea Bay' (c.1806), if there are no signs of high talent, she nevertheless succeeds in setting her mood to the sea's melancholy:

> The restless waves that lave the shore,
>   Joining the tide's tumultuous roar;
> In hollow murmurs seem to say —
>   Peace is not found at Swansea Bay.

The third of the trio, though she cannot match the length of residence of the other two, nevertheless spent some twenty-seven years in Wales. Felicia Hemans was born Browne in Liverpool in 1793, but settled with her family at Gwrych, near Abergele, in 1800. Her short life of forty-two years was soon involved with the making of books: her *Juvenile Poems* (1808) came out when she was no more than fourteen and a second volume, *The Domestic Affections and Other Poems*, in 1812. From 1809 she lived at Bronwylfa, her brother's house near St. Asaph, and her marriage, which took her briefly out of Wales, ended in separation in 1818. Amongst the several plays, largely unsuccessful, and the many volumes of verse she produced was one called *Welsh Melodies* (1821), though the proportion this represents in her collected *Poems* is small. Even the briefest reading of her work reveals, indeed that, despite a brief flurry with the Eisteddfod in 1822, her interests were internationally Romantic; the wide range of her feminine sensibility and her identification with chivalry and facile emotion made her one of the most popular poets of her day. If her sweetness and fluency are distasteful to subsequent generations, that is partly a matter of the tastes of her own age, partly the

30. Felicia Hemans. Portrait by W.E. West

31. Gerard Manley Hopkins as a boy.
Watercolour by A.E. Hopkins, 1859

lack in her writing of the personal involvement expected of a poet in the twentieth century.

Two of the women we have been discussing, then, may reasonably be called 'Little Englanders'. Swansea was, in the early nineteenth century, an 'English' watering-place: Abergele and St. Asaph were not much more than Romantic foregrounds for a dream that began with 'England'. But such a distinction becomes increasingly difficult. The line to be drawn between Ann of Swansea, let us say, and Walter Savage Landor, who may have lived in Swansea for as many as ten years (certainly writing *Gebir* and 'Rose Aylmer' there) becomes a hedging matter. Should we accept, for example, the *Rhaiadr Gwy* (1840) of the long-resident schoolmaster Daniel Carter but not the Welsh topographical poems of a train of visiting poets from Luke Booker and Shelley to Matthew Arnold and Tennyson? And what of Gerard Manley Hopkins's three years (1874-77) at St. Beuno's College near St. Asaph? It is the more difficult to dismiss such a company because there is clearly a feedback from some of them. If there is more than a doubt about the claim that Montgomery Castle was George Herbert's place of birth, there is none about the influence of *The Temple* on the writing of Henry Vaughan. And Hopkins, in learning enough Welsh to command some of the tight metrical forms of Welsh prosody, not merely made of English poetry something that was temporarily more exciting: he also influenced Dylan Thomas, years later, and brought *his* poetry into a relationship with the tradition in Welsh which his own ignorance of the language must necessarily have precluded. It is possible, therefore, to see too rigid a definition of the term 'Anglo-Welsh' as ultimately sterile.

Similarly, in the doubt that fogs this field, we are bound to hover uncertainly over a work like James Motley's *Tales of the Cymry* (1848), a book which consists of half a dozen long poems, amongst them 'Cwm Annwn' and 'The Ceffyl-y-Dwfr'. Motley was an Englishman born at Osmondthorpe Hall near Leeds, the son of a woolstapler who attended Call Lane Independent Chapel. After Cambridge he became a civil engineer and came to South Wales to supervise his father's ultimately unsuccessful undertakings, ironworks at Maesteg and coal-mines round Llangynwyd. The Preface to *Tales of the Cymry* is dated from Abercrave perhaps no more than a few weeks before James Motley sailed for Borneo to work for a Dutch mining company. He was to meet his death there in a tribal uprising in 1859. What he writes in his poems about Wales is full-bloodedly Romantic: he embraces the Welsh tradition in a way that makes most of his contemporaries amongst native writers look self-conscious and half-hearted. Such fervour is indeed characteristic of incomers and exiles, in descending order: a Celtophile Englishman like James Kenward of Smethwick (*For Cambria*, 1868) exceeds in matter and manner the cooler tone of an exile like Mrs. Bowen, the author of *Ystradffin* (1839), a long, topographical excursion supported by detailed notes, and the more sporadic Romanticism of a second-generation Welshwoman like Anne Powell, who published *Clifton, Caractacus, Boadicea and Other Pieces* in Bristol in 1821. There is no evidence at present that any of the writers just mentioned gave a lead to those who qualify more obviously by both blood and residence for our consideration, but it is nevertheless scarcely possible to disown Kenward, for example, who claims fifteen years' study of Welsh history and tradition, and to include Felicia Hemans and Ann of Swansea, who were never interested enough to pursue them beyond the first mile.

Moreover, we cannot but be conscious that just outside the range discussed loom other far more important literary figures whose family origins lay in Wales. Amongst poets who can be discerned are John Donne, Thomas Traherne, Christopher Smart, Arthur Hugh Clough and William Morris and amongst novelists George Meredith. There is a second rank too, not more distant than the first but less generally renowned. Ebenezer Jones – not to be confused with Ernest Charles Jones, the Chartist poet, who was also Welsh by parentage – published *Studies of Sensation and Event* 1843. Born in Islington in 1820 of a Welsh father, he could not return to Wales with his family: instead he and his brother Sumner felt compelled to extend their wearisome days in a City counting-house. Dante Gabriel Rossetti remarked on the "vivid, disorderly power" of a poet whose struggles, at evenings and week-ends, to find the energy to write gradually became weaker.

Beyond the Joneses and the other progeny of expatriate Welshmen may be discerned another small and shadowy group, that of the entirely English poets of renown who interested themselves in the literature and traditions of Wales. Thomas Gray and Matthew Arnold are the most easily recognisable of these, and the latter's lectures *On the Study of Celtic Literature*, published in 1867, the last year of his Professorship of Poetry at Oxford, were probably the most influential from such a platform throughout the century. If we find his attribution of 'style' to the poetry of the *Gogynfeirdd* and his implication that the Celtic spirit could not (and perhaps should not) survive in a modern reality too didactic, at least the exhortation towards a more general interest in Celtic studies was a plain statement of the value to be derived from them. His prime examples of Welsh poetry were far from contemporary: indeed, what he wrote was irrelevant to the tradition either in Welsh or in English of his own day. But to take any cultural aspect of Wales as a *serious* ingredient of the English tradition was in itself something that had not happened (except in the philosophical fiction of Peacock) for centuries. The *reality* for Welshmen in the mid-nineteenth century had too often been an English attitude which was either patronising or jeering.

Goronva Camlann, whose very pseudonym suggests an age that is over, terminated and irrecoverable, demonstrates his resentment of this in the Preface to his *Lays from the Cimbric Lyre* (1846). His aim, he says, is to rescue "here an ancient legend and there a living characteristic . . . from under the threatening train of steam-engines and schoolmasters". The "eye of unity" with which Shakespeare, Spenser and the writers of the Elizabethan age saw their Britain is shut as with a cataract.

> In whichever of the three kingdoms a poor Celt may have been born, he can scarcely take up an English newspaper, but he finds himself and his birth and kin either disparaged, or by implication, annihilated. A stranger to our history might infer from the tone of our periodical literature, that these same Saxons either found our island as desert as that of Robinson Crusoe, or exterminated all previous inhabitants; or at least that they possessed some qualities so brilliant as to render them alone in Great Britain thenceforward deserving of mention.

The Welsh had made the mistake, not merely of having a different language and an inferior history (as a *conquered* people) but of having a Church whose hierarchy was determined that it should be *of England*. *Brad y Llyfrau Gleision* (The Treachery of the Blue Books) was less than twelve months away.

It will be apparent to the reader that in recent pages poetry has been discussed largely in terms of the social origin or attitude of those who wrote it. Such an emphasis may seem strange in a literary history: it occurs mainly because discussion of the poets named, from the seventeenth century onwards, is vitally affected by the issue of confidence and a viable tradition. By and large these poets lacked the gift which would transcend their origin and status. It should also be apparent that the tradition in which Anglo-Welsh writing began – with the Tudor glory, and behind it the line of Welsh princes going back to Brutus the Trojan, with the seniority of centuries that that implied – had all but disintegrated. Progressively from the middle of the seventeenth century versifiers in English, themselves not men of outstanding parts, were writing from a Wales that was unconfident, poor, provincial and second-rate: they partook of the enfeebled spirit, the servility of the times to which they belonged. The malaise

32. Lady Charlotte Guest. Portrait by W. Walker after R. Buckner, 1852

affected the whole nation. Those who spoke Welsh and wrote in it, by committing themselves to the Cymmrodorion Society or one of its rivals, or to the Eisteddfod as it began to develop in the early years of the nineteenth century, attempted to keep going the dignity of the earlier tradition, but their emphasis was mainly antiquarian: even with the help and encouragement of converts from the immigrant industrial plutocracy like Lady Charlotte Guest and Lady Llanover they rarely faced up to making it contemporary. Those who were out of touch with Welsh antiquarian institutions were affected in spirit both by being educated in English and by the spectacle of a social pyramid whose upper quartile was dominated by English-speakers. A sense of inferiority became deeply ingrained in the great majority of the Welsh-speaking population. Those who spoke and wrote only English, of whatever class, were farther than ever from a Welsh tradition and disinclined, except in rare cases of bitterness, to use it: English verse models were inevitably to hand, and those of the simplest: the determination to develop even an occasional Welsh subject became progressively feebler. The enthusiasms of English Romantics in no way affected this situation: their lack of inhibition ignored the current social values. Even when a Hopkins, coming from outside, created an English poetry which had been structurally and texturally affected by experience of the Welsh tradition, it revitalised Anglo-Welsh writing in the only way it could have done – long after its own time, in another century.

Before we leave the still-declining nineteenth century scene, however, it must be said that there had been or were a few poets who by ability, reading or a temperament that, by making them mobile, freed them from the detritus of social prejudice, had raised themselves above the literary scree we have been describing. Two of these belong to the eighteenth century, when the slide was not so bad that it could not still get worse. The first was John Dyer (1699-1757).

Dyer was of Aberglasne in Carmarthenshire, the son of a solicitor. He became a painter and travelled a good deal in Italy. Indeed, he was little known as a writer before the appearance of 'Grongar Hill' in 1726. This, his best-known poem, came early in the canon of genuinely descriptive and topographical verse and it is highly likely that, in this regard, he had been influenced by his study of the painter Claude. There is about

33. John Dyer, poet and artist. Line engraving by J. Barker

34. Grongar Hill. From Henry Gastineau, *South Wales Illustrated* 1829

'Grongar Hill' (though it opens much less impressively than it ends) a certainty of language which, while in no sense peculiar or original, is solidly part of its descriptive purpose: it is simple and direct and its exactness can still be gauged in part by anyone who climbs the hill today. The conclusion is one with it in knowledge and feeling:

> Be full, ye courts, be great who will;
> Search for Peace with all your skill;
> Open wide the lofty door,
> Seek her on the marble floor:
> In vain ye search, she is not there;
> In vain ye search the domes of Care!
> Grass and flowers Quiet treads,
> On the meads and mountain-heads,
> Along with Pleasure, close allied,
> Ever by each other's side:
> And often, by the murmuring rill,
> Hears the thrush, while all is still,
> Within the groves of Grongar Hill.

The rather insistent end-rhymes are, in the first six lines of the quotation, linked by repetition into a kind of hammering which is the antithesis of Peace: the slower rhythm that begins with "Grass and flowers" is marked by an increasing number of 'l' sounds and the extra line which concludes provides an additional echo of this onomatopoeic calm. How calculated this was it is impossible to say. But that the Towy valley, through Dyer's poem, had achieved a measure of fame is attested by John Lloyd's lines quoted earlier. Dyer also published 'The Ruins of Rome' in 1740 and 'The Fleece' in 1757 – the

35. Evan Lloyd, cleric and satirist. Engraving
by G. Marchi after J. Berridge

latter full of memories of Wales. He was ordained in 1741 and ten years later became
vicar of Coningsby in Lincolnshire.

The second poet who made something of a mark in his own time was Evan Lloyd of
Fron Dderw, Bala (1734-76), whom Garrick called "a man of genius"– admittedly in a
letter in which he was seeking preferment for Lloyd. Educated at Ruthin School and
Jesus College, Oxford, he entered the Church and became curate at Redriff
(Rotherhithe) – a name that echoes in the work of David Jones two centuries later.
Always rather an odd Churchman and later the absentee vicar of Llanfair Dyffryn
Clwyd, Lloyd was a wit, a hater of pomposity and undue gravity and, like John Aubrey
in the previous century, a man with a wide circle of friends, including David Garrick
and John Wilkes. Needless to say, his satirical pen made and sought out enemies –
reviewers, critics, Methodists and reformers, fops, the Government of the day: William
Price of Rhiwlas had him in prison once for caricaturing him as 'Libidinoso'. Whether
Dr. Johnson appreciated the following lines from *The Powers of the Pen* (1766,
reprinted 1768) does not appear, but such combativeness was bound to make for Lloyd
a contemporary name of a sort:

> A *Dictionary's* small Pretence
> To warrant such high Insolence –
> A *learned Mummy* might explain
> (If you but well embalm the Brain)
> *Words* and *their various Sense* – might shew
> A modern *Critic* means – a Foe.

This was the most successful of Evan Lloyd's four long poems and though, in the end,
like most satirists, he himself is hammered inextricably into his own time, there is no
doubt that he had a natural talent for writing and a gift for the telling phrase.

The third writer, and the least distinctive of the three to achieve some personal
reputation, was Lewis Morris (1833-1907), great-grandson of his namesake *Llywelyn*

36. Sir Lewis Morris. Portrait by Carey Morris, 1906

Ddu o Fôn. Born at Carmarthen and educated at the Queen Elizabeth Grammar School there, at Cowbridge and Sherborne Schools and at Jesus College, Oxford, he had a brilliant academic career, was called to the bar in 1861, served University College, Aberystwyth in various honorary offices from 1878, and was knighted for his services to higher education. Unfortunately, despite his friendship with Tennyson, his verse is less distinguished. Three volumes of *Songs of Two Worlds* (1872-75) were followed by *The Epic of Hades* (1876-77). Morris's *Collected Works*, published in 1891, sold eleven thousand copies within five years. His poems, however, demonstrate, almost infallibly, the smooth, expected word: such fluency leaves on a modern reader very little impression. Regrettably, too, his approach to Wales – though he used Welsh subjects often enough – was marked by the kind of English Romanticism Motley or Kenward would have called 'pale'. 'Wild Wales', (for example) has a title Borrovian in origin, but the poem, from Morris's pen, loses all the life and astringency evoked from the land Borrow visited.

Nevertheless, 615 pages of verse, mostly double-columned, can scarcely be written off in the same breath as the minuscule offerings of many of his predecessors. Here and there something different breaks through the smooth surface: 'David Gwyn', for instance, is surprisingly jagged and unformed – and in consequence emotional – and in *Songs of Britain* (1887) there are a few pieces whose sparer structure compels greater verbal precision. 'In Pembrokeshire, 1886', for example, – a poem he wrote after being defeated in a Parliamentary election in the County – has glimmerings of a more individual achievement:

> The swift train swept with rhythmic tune,
> By endless pastures hurrying down,
> White farm, lone chapel, castled town,
> Then, fringed with weed, the salt lagune

And last the land-locked haven blue,
Thin-sown with monstrous works of war,
And on the sweet salt air I knew
Faint sounds of cheering from afar.

Confident in his own natural ability and in his qualities as a popular educator Lewis Morris may have been: confident in his heritage from Wales he was not.

IX The Nationalist Revival

If Anglo-Welsh poetry had by the nineteenth century an apologetic sound, creative writing in prose was much younger and even less confident. Since the mid-eighteenth century Wales had become increasingly a Nonconformist commonwealth in *Welsh*, and the people left outside that commonwealth – the few resident gentry, ironmasters and their servants, clerics, masters of Church schools, incomers and social climbers – were both few in proportion and, in most cases, alienated from their traditional heritage. Such important writing as there was came from 'men of affairs' who had left Wales, and these were far fewer in number than in the Tudor heyday. The most distinctive group were London Welshmen whose activities might be described as widely political rather than antiquarian – such as David Williams of Eglwysilan, Caerphilly, who wrote a *Treatise on Education* (1774) and *Letters on Political Liberty* (1782), and Richard Price of Llangeinor, whose *Observations on the Nature of Civil Liberty* (1776), with other pamphlets political, philosophical and actuarial, made him a man whose significance to the rebel colonists in America has never yet been sufficiently echoed in this country. Robert Owen of Newtown, too, though his career took him to Manchester and Lanark rather than London, was another whose progressive political and social thinking was a rationalisation of the 'democracy' to be found in Welsh-speaking Wales. His *A New View of Society* (1813), to name only one of his many

37. Robert Owen's Ideal Village, Orbiston, Lanarkshire

38. An Archdruid in his Judicial Habit.
Coloured aquatint from S.R. Meyrick
and C.H. Smith, *The Costume of the
Original Inhabitants of the British Isles*, 1815

works – for this is not the place even to summarise his achievements in factory reform, distributive co-operation and the setting up of nursery schools – was the beginning of much social and democratic thinking that is still reaching fruition in the twentieth century. Again, the philosophical writings of Sir Henry Jones (1852-1922), though mainly the product of his long professorship at Glasgow University, arose from a genuinely Welsh background in Denbighshire. Much more accidental, in the Welsh context, were the African writings of H.M. Stanley (1841-1904). As John Rowlands of Denbigh he had not known much more of Wales than the conditions inside the St.Asaph workhouse.

Meanwhile antiquarian writing – though it burst out more confidently in periodicals like John Humffreys Parry's *Cambro-Briton* and occasionally in essays in English on Welsh institutions set for Eisteddfod competitions (two by Walter Davies (*Gwallter Mechain*) published in 1822 and one by William Jones on *The Character of the Welsh as a Nation* (1841) come to mind) – had fallen on evil days. "An almost unrelieved lunatic darkness", writes Stuart Piggott in *The Druids* (1968) had fallen on Celtic philology since the time of Edward Lhwyd, and the characteristic works of the late eighteenth and early nineteenth centuries were those on Druidical lore of Edward Davies and Rowland Jones – an esoteric tradition that was handed on through such as Dr. William Price of Llantrisant and *Morien* (Owen Morgan of Ystradyfodwg) well into the twentieth century. Indeed, some of the best work in the field of antiquarian and genealogical studies was done towards the end of the nineteenth century by adopted Welshmen like G.T. Clark in Glamorgan and Arthur Neobard Palmer in Wrexham.

The revival earlier of a more contemporary Welsh *spirit*, visible politically in the activities of Michael D. Jones and 'S.R.', had not been entirely without echo in the writings of Welshmen in English. Sir Thomas Phillips, born at Clydach below Brynmawr, had become a London barrister. Irritated, even out of his Churchmanship, by the Report of the Church Commissioners in 1847 which became known as *Brad y Llyfrau Gleision* (The Treachery of the Blue Books), he published in 1849 *Wales, the Language, Social Conditions, Moral Character and Religious Opinions of the People*

39. Rees Gronow, Parisian dandy, duellist and chronicler. Engraving by J.C. Armitage

considered in their relation to Education. This, despite its clumsy title, was an effective counter-attack, bespeaking some recovery of confidence. Arthur James Johnes's *An Essay on the Causes which have produced Dissent from the Established Church in the Principality of Wales* (1872) represents another stage in the process. Johnes was by profession a county court judge, the son of the landed family of Garthmyl, Montgomeryshire, and we ought perhaps to recognise, in his book and in Sir Thomas Phillips's, and indeed in the attack made by Benjamin Hall, Lord Llanover, on the Bishop of St. David's (for his treatment of the foundation of Christ College, Brecon, then in desperate plight) in his *Letter to the Archbishop of Canterbury* (1851), the first signs of a lack of sympathy for the Church Establishment in Wales amongst professional men and the new gentry. The older gentry, in their more cosmopolitan and absentee guise, were represented only by the Neath-born but Eton-educated Rees Gronow, whose *Reminiscences of Captain Gronow* were published in four series between 1862 and 1866. At Waterloo without permission in order to serve under Picton, Gronow later became a captain: as a civilian dandy in his later years he watched the world from his Paris window with sharp eyes. Amongst *Diaries* not published in their owners' lifetime we may note that of Robert Morris, the quixotic and peculiar son of the coppermaster who gave Morriston its name. From 1772 to 1774 he was abroad in disgrace, trying to consummate in marriage the elopement he had brought off with the child to whom he was supposedly guardian. Like Evan Lloyd, he too was a friend of John Wilkes.

The build-up of nationalist politics towards the end of the nineteenth century produced, of course, prolific and influential oratory from Thomas Edward Ellis and David Lloyd George (the speeches of the former were published in 1912 and the *War Memoirs* of the latter from 1933 onwards). But neither they, nor Henry Richard, the 'Apostle of Peace', are our concern here. Out of a tremendous activity in Welsh what reached publication in English was a proportion small but influential. Owen M. Edwards's *Wales* (1901), in the *Story of the Nations* series, added to the impact of the scholarly labours of John Rhys, who had revived the study of Welsh philology with his *Lectures* (1877) and had gone on to create a new 'model' of early Welsh history in many published works, the most popularly-pointed of which was probably *The Welsh People* (1900), written in collaboration with David Brynmor-Jones. That that 'model' is now obsolete does not in any way invalidate the scale of the achievement.

X The Nineteenth Century Novel

The importance of political, academic, philosophical and other writings here, however, – and many more could have been added – is only to afford a contrast with the general poverty of the creative prose works in English during the nineteenth century. Novels of a sort there had been, even before 1800 – like Mrs. Agnes Maria Bennett's *Anna, or Memoirs of a Welch Heiress* (1785), Mrs. Gunning's *Delves: A Welsh Tale* (1796), and Herbert Lawrence's *Contemplative Man: or, The History of Christopher Crab Esq., of North Wales* (1771). But these were by authors of slender Welsh connection who used Wales as a land of Romance or found it easy to transfer their philosophical and aesthetic ideas to a setting impenetrable by most of their readers. Essentially, no doubt, the approach of Thomas Love Peacock was little different: the Welsh backgrounds of *Headlong Hall* (1816) and *Crotchet Castle* (1831) were important chiefly for their exemplification of natural beauty within the context of Peacock's philosophical and satirical intention – as a terrestrial paradise in which his beliefs could work themselves out. Yet his attitude to his Welsh characters is contradictory: although his characterisation is essentially comic and superficial, Wales was for him, as David Gallon has put it, "a beautiful country inhabited by unbearable people". In other words, society had hopelessly corrupted the innocence fostered by natural beauty. But personal factors have to be accounted for here, as rarely with earlier writers: Peacock was married to a Welshwoman and his daughter, before she went off with Wallis the painter, was married to George Meredith, himself of Welsh extraction. Against this, however, must stand the important fact that in *The Misfortunes of Elphin* (1829) Peacock did Wales the great service of using traditions embodied in the Welsh language to create a narrative which, while it links tales not integrally connected and omits or adds wherever the author's Rousseau-istic ideas of

40. Thomas Love Peacock. Portrait by Henry Wallis, 1858

41. Sker House, on the Glamorgan coast

education indicated the need for 'improvement', is nevertheless a pioneering work that has been very little followed.

While it has to be acknowledged that all the significant writing in the field of the novel before the end of the century – or almost all of it – came from individuals who were either non-Welsh or much less resident than Peacock, it is worth pointing out that R.D. Blackmore's *The Maid of Sker* (1872) is the work of a man with a Welsh mother who spent many years of his childhood at Nottage Court in Glamorgan: in it, and through the narrator, Davy Llewellyn, he sounds a note of Welsh 'superiority' which had rarely been heard since the early seventeenth century. Charles Kingsley, who also had Glamorgan connections, in 1857 published *Two Years Ago*, a story set in the Beddgelert region. Other established writers made an incursion or two: W.H.G. Kingston published *Eldol the Druid* in 1874 and Mrs. Gaskell wrote two short stories – 'The Doom of the Griffiths' and 'The Well of Penmorfa' – which probably date from 1858. But the most Peacockian of all the books which followed *Elphin*, not in its Welsh source material but in its attempt to use the landscape of Snowdonia to point up an essentially Romantic philosophy, is Theodore Watts-Dunton's *Aylwin* (1898). The book's sub-title, *The Renascence of Wonder*, marks out the ground and the theme is doubly insured by its evocation of gypsy life and character (after Borrow). It is perhaps a pity that that descendant of the Flintshire Evanses who became the English novelist George Eliot visited Wales only once – in September 1875, when the journey "was altogether unfortunate on account of excessive rain"; otherwise we might have had from an outside witness a novel more socially observant and closer to the ethos of a real Welsh community.

42. 'Twm Sion Catti Offering a Horse for Sale at Llandovery Fair'. Illustration by Edward Salter from T.J. Llewelyn Prichard, *Twm Sion Catti* (Llanidloes, 1873)

No doubt other novels with Welsh settings are not hard to find, and there are a few, like Tobias Smollett's *Roderick Random* (1748) and *The Adventures of Humphrey Clinker* (1771), and George Meredith's *Evan Harrington* (1860) which incorporate Welsh characters. What matters for our purpose, however, is the contrasting poverty of the writing in English by the native Welsh. Thomas Jeffery Llewelyn Prichard's *The Adventures and Vagaries of Twm Shon Catti* (1828) has some claim to be called the first novel in English from Wales: but in truth it is, particularly in its first version, a ragbag of a book, in which Prichard, re-using his *Cambro-Briton* contributions, is concerned, within a rough framework afforded by Twm's adventures, to present as much Welsh traditional material as possible – from flummery to costume to courting in bed and back again. Really a miscellany, relatively undeveloped from the monthly-journal concept, it is both full of anti-English feeling and yet directed towards the English taste for *grotesquerie*.

Twm Shon Catti's deficiencies notwithstanding, it was some years before any successors appeared. The only novelist worthy of the name who began to publish in mid-century was Rhoda Broughton (1840-1920). A clergyman's daughter, born near Denbigh, she was brought up in Staffordshire but lived in North Wales for a number of years after her father's death. Among her many books – and she produced one every two years or so – the best-known are *Cometh up as a Flower* and *Not Wisely But Too Well* (both 1867), *Red as a Rose is She* (1870), *Belinda* (1883), *Dr. Cupid* (1886), *A Waif's Progress* (1905) and *The Devil and the Deep Sea* (1910). All of these, and a number of others, ran through many editions; their determinedly romantic form was nevertheless supported by writing of high quality. The comparative looseness of *Cometh up as a Flower*, for example, becomes in *Belinda* a very tight control of

43. Mallt Williams, novelist, nationalist and
feminist. Photograph from Thomas
Stephens, *Cymru: Heddyw ac Yfory*, 1908

structure, conversation and incident, coupled with an extremely small cast (some of whom are dogs), by means of which intensity of feeling can be made to last the novel long. All Rhoda Broughton's earlier books were written in Wales but her natural milieu was the Staffordshire of her childhood. Her popularity in her day was no less than that of Mrs. Henry Wood and Wilkie Collins and her wit and sense of humour give her an advantage in those respects over both.

What she has to say about Wales is unfortunately little, in contrast with the work of the incomer Anne Beale, whose sketches and character portraits in *The Vale of Towey* (1844), probably influenced in form by Mary Russell Mitford's *Our Village* and *Belford Regis*, have the mark of a writer well disposed and long enough resident to be capable of a response to the comments of travellers. It is interesting to note that this was the form that commended itself to the majority of unconfident native prose writers at the end of the century.

Upwards of twenty years passed between Rhoda Broughton's first book and the appearance of anything faintly comparable by other Welsh writers. Then, when novels came, the impetus was partly a nationalistic one – the sisters Mallt and Gwenffrida Williams, under the pseudonym *Y Dau Gwynne*, wrote *One of the Royal Celts* (1889) and *A Maid of Cymru* (1901) – and partly a shy but swelling desire to present Welsh life and society for approval outside. An unprecedented number of prose works published in the last two decades of the century have this for their main purpose, amongst them the Rev. David Davies's *Echoes from the Welsh Hills* (1883) and *John Vaughan and his Friends* (1897), Eleazer Roberts's *Owen Rees* (1893), John Thomas's *To the Angel's Chair* (1897) and John Bufton's *Gwen Penri: A Welsh Idyll* (1899). *Owen Tanat* (1897) by Robert Rees (the pseudonym of Alfred Neobard Palmer, the incomer turned local historian) is probably more successful than any of them.

44. Cover from *The Red Dragon*

Two matters, probably linked, call for comment here. The first is the belatedness of this prose development, the second the frequency of the use of pseudonyms. *Red Dragon*, edited between 1883 and 1885 by the indefatigable Charles Wilkins of Merthyr, author of *The History of the Literature of Wales from 1300 to 1650* (1884), was the only magazine in English published in Wales in the eighties: a perusal of its monthly issues reveals the absence of Welsh subject matter from the novels serialised, the infrequency of verse except that submitted by pseudonymous contributors (H. Elvet Lewis is an interesting exception) and a heavy emphasis on Welsh historical biography, sketches of past ways of life in Wales and antiquarian *minutiae*. Wilkins wrote a not inconsiderable part of each issue himself: he was plainly seeking to create an Anglo-Welsh ethos without the help of any sufficient public interest or confidence. For the vast mass of English-speaking newcomers who had already moved into south-east Wales since 1870 his appeal to a Welshness in English was altogether too early. And the unconfident native Welsh were little more ready.

Nevertheless, individual writers of greater importance, if still pseudonymous, were soon to appear. The first was Allen Raine. Born Anne Adalisa Evans and surnamed Puddicombe after marriage, she wrote eleven novels in all – the earliest were *A Welsh Singer* (1897), *Torn Sails* (1898), *By Berwen Banks* (1899) and *Garthowen* (1900) – many of which, having run through a number of immediate editions, were reprinted again after an interval of years. It has been the fashion since the thirties of this century to denigrate the work of Allen Raine because it was popular and Romantic in the humanly sentimental sense, (a denigration which other, more esoteric, kinds of Romanticism are allowed to escape): but, fashions apart, a literary history must recognise a qualitative improvement in any mode of writing. In comparison with the woodenness of much of what previous writers had contributed (Rhoda Broughton always excepted) Allen Raine's work exhibits fluency itself: the Cardiganshire background, entirely new to English readers (who had been regaled previously, for the

45. Allen Raine (Anne Adaliza Puddicombe),
    novelist. Portrait from *Wales*, 1911

46. Owen Rhoscomyl (Arthur Owen Vaughan:
    real name Robert Scourfield Mills),
    commander of Rimington's Guides,
    novelist and historian

most part, on North Wales), is treated with warmth: history, where it appears (as in *Hearts of Wales*, 1905), is not entirely incredible: the plotting is good and the conversations, though not invariably well managed, are an advance on the efforts of previous writers brought up within the boundaries of Wales.

Slightly earlier in the field, though seeking a different public, was Owen Rhoscomyl (Arthur Owen Vaughan, 1863?-1919). An adventurer who captained Rimington's Guides in the Boer War, his real name was Robert Scourfield Mills; who was of Pembrokeshire stock but associated himself with the Vale of Clwyd. Probably he was the first Welshman who spoke only English to demonstrate in his prose writing a direct and unashamed patriotism, and his *Flamebearers of Welsh History* (1905), if much more zealous than professional, had a profound influence on the young generation. Some years before this he had begun to write books to which heroic action is the key: *The Jewel of Ynys Galon* (1895) was followed by *The White Rose of Arno* and at least four other stories. After the success of *Flamebearers* his later books – beginning with *Old Fireproof* (1906) and *Vronina* (1907) – were signed (Captain) Owen Vaughan. Amongst his last endeavours was a play, which he wrote in collaboration with Lord Howard de Walden, called *The Children of Don* (1912). If most of his books can be catalogued as 'For boys, young and old', they are nevertheless a Welsh contribution to the honourable school of Ballantyne and Henty, and the impossibility, in the later twentieth century, of reproducing their attitudes in new writing should be enough to secure their historical value for modern readers.

But Owen Rhoscomyl, Allen Raine and their like were not as it happened, the

47. 'A Stopper'. Illustration by Henry Alken from Nimrod, *The Chase, The Turf and the Road*, 1837

harbingers of the Anglo-Welsh writing that was to begin with the First World War. To explain why this was so we need to go back to the beginning of the nineteenth century, to a kind of prose writing much more common amongst the Welsh than the construction of novels. Its chief manifestation was the sketch – the short description from life, if occasionally a good way from it. The most gifted and least typical practitioner in this field was one of the earliest: 'Nimrod' (Charles James Apperley, born in 1779 at Plas Gronow, Wrexham, earlier the house of Elihu Yale) was by wish a gentleman but in fact penniless. In *The Life of a Sportsman* (1842) and *Memoirs of the Life of John Mytton* (1837) he wrote of that "happy-go-lucky, ten-thousand-a-year world" in which he existed on sufferance. The popularity of his contributions to *The Sporting Magazine*, many of which were based on the squirarchical life of the Montgomeryshire-Shropshire border, did not save him from debt and temporary exile in 1830 on the Continent.

More commonly, however, the Welshman's sketch was either traditional and topographical, a faint answer to the chorus of travelling diarists – like the journalist Richard Richards's *Miscellaneous Poems and Pen-and-Ink Sketches* (1868) – or, as the century wore on, traditional and sentimental evocations of particular places and people, often presented as occupational stereotypes or portraits of Welsh society. There was a passion for biography, much of it taking its origin from a pious care for the reputation of the Dissenting Fathers, as in John Evans's *Cambro-British Biography* (1820). Thomas Stephens, the Merthyr chemist, already well known for his Eisteddfod dissertation *The Literature of the Kymry* (1849), pressed forward the wider aspects of this biographical writing with a series of articles which were published in book form long after his death in *Welshmen from the Earliest Times to Llywelyn* (1901). Right up to 1950, when Wyn Griffith's book *The Welsh* appeared, the idea of the brief collective portrait had some vogue, but this was probably the last date at which the Welsh were sufficiently unknown and recognisably different to excite the curiosity of an English readership.

A great deal of the writing in this vein had constituted very amateur history and, literarily, the creative element had rarely been other than small. But with the appearance in 1889 of the lawyer T. Marchant Williams's *Land of My Fathers* a more confident and imaginative note was struck. Amongst the books which followed may be mentioned *In the Land of the Harp and Feathers* (1896) by Alfred Thomas, Zachary Mathers' *Tales from the Welsh Hills* (1909), three of the stories in which had been awarded prizes at the National Eisteddfod of 1902 by Sir Lewis Morris, J.O. Francis's *The Legend of the Welsh* (1924), a reprint of newspaper articles, and – less popular and more seriously historical – Blanche Devereux's *Star of Mercia* (1922).

These small fruits were to turn sour, however. The tradition of English *superiority*, deeply entrenched amongst the socially ambitious in Wales, shot its last public bolts just before the First World War. 'Draig Glas' (Arthur Tyssilio Johnson) published *The Perfidious Welshman* in 1910: it is not much more than a catalogue of stale gibes and scurrilous abuse, without benefit of any wit beyond that of the schoolboy. Amongst hints for the 'English visitor' one of the less offensive runs as follows:

> When in conversation with a Welshman, and he turns his back on you, or looks in
> the other direction, and begins whistling, don't be offended, because it is his way of
> looking you in the face. He knows no better manners.

This was replied to by 'An Englishman' in *The Welshman's Reputation* (1911) and by 'Fluellyn' in a *Reply* of the same year, while the original indictment was reinforced, with more style and considerably less abuse, by T.W.H. Crosland in *Taffy Was a Welshman* (1912). Commenting on the great increase of the Welsh population of London, Crosland writes:

> Being Englishmen, we should catch cold if we didn't have our necks under
> somebody's hot foot, and it might as well be the Welsh as anybody else.

The mainspring of this book's attack is unquestionably dislike of Lloyd George and the new turn his increasing ascendancy was giving to Liberal policy. All this, however, might be dismissed as a silly and unworthy attempt to capture the 'prejudice' market were it not that it very probably tipped the wink to a much more considerable writer, Caradoc Evans, and through him helped to point a direction for Anglo-Welsh prose writing for some twenty-five or thirty years.

XI Changes in Society

The history of Anglo-Welsh writing in the twentieth century cannot seriously be undertaken, however, without some consideration of the vast social and educational changes that had overtaken Wales from the middle of the nineteenth century onwards. Two aspects of these, above all, must be described. The first, and by far the more important, was the immigration into what had been the strongly Welsh bastion of the Silures in south-east Wales of thousands of Englishmen and their families, all drawn there by the mines and steelworks of the region's industrial Klondyke. The settlement of strangers in Gwent and the eastern half of Glamorgan represented by 1911 a percentage of the population not less than forty and assimilation of the newcomers by a very recently established Welsh-speaking industrial society proved impossible. In no more than a few decades English, already the language of the law, of commerce, of education and social betterment, was the only language both of large homogeneous groups of working people who no longer had any need to learn Welsh and of the easily discouraged amongst former Welsh-speakers. The psychological effect of this change, particularly on Welsh-speaking parents, was tremendous: if they were to do their best for their children, they began to argue, they must educate them in the English language, by means of which alone advancement was possible. The conviction that this was necessary was forced by the new attitude of the times even upon those brought up within the Nonconformist tradition, to whom the older pro-English snobbery had never appealed.

This linguistic pressure was compounded by a second development – the advent of secondary schooling for all who could qualify academically for it. The new County or Grammar Schools established under the Welsh Intermediate Education Act of 1889 and the wider Education Act of 1902 (as secured by 'the Welsh revolt') were at first very small, often containing no more than a hundred pupils, while the majority of children of secondary school age still languished in all-age primary schools: but the door was nevertheless open to children of the lower middle and working classes, who would be educated as adolescents *entirely in English* at a time when Welsh, even if spoken by their parents, was disappearing from their environment of playground and street. Here, then, was a deepening well of so-far-untapped talent in the English language, one which took its waters from a region which, as early as 1890, had contained more than half the entire population of Wales.

One or two generalisations may be made about Anglo-Welsh writers of the first twentieth century draught in the light of this historical prelude. Glyn Jones, himself one of the writers he categorises, proffers, in his book *The Dragon Has Two Tongues* (1968), the opinion that 'the talent belt' in Welsh society was previously to be found in that section of it which was Welsh-speaking, radical in politics and Nonconformist in religion, and that when a family from that 'belt' began to speak English at home the appearance of an Anglo-Welsh writer became a distinct possibility. These were the people, whether their fathers were colliers, teachers, steelworkers, small shopkeepers or ministers of religion, who would rarely, if ever, have found a place at a grammar school of the older sort and who would not have been admitted to university before 1872. Socially they represented a class from which writers in English had in previous centuries emerged in very small numbers indeed, but from which their contemporaries, writers in Welsh and eisteddfod competitors, came almost exclusively.

48. Idris Davies with his sister and uncle
outside 16 Field Street, Rhymney, *c.* 1908-09

This first batch of Anglo-Welsh writers had one strength which most of their successors were to be without: they were, if not themselves capable of writing and speaking Welsh, in touch with older members of their own families (grandparents, parents, uncles, aunts) who spoke the language, and had means of knowing and remembering, from the formative years of childhood, what the Welsh way of life was or had been. This was a position very different from that of the great majority of Anglo-Welsh writers before 1900, whose exclusion from Welshness had been a matter of class and background as well as language. It is a position that must be borne in mind when the question of the exploitation of the Welsh heritage is discussed.

It is possible, too, – if now scarcely provable – that the uninhibited eloquence of older Welsh speakers – what is too often loosely called the *hwyl* – had its echo in the extraordinary richness and profusion of language which was common to this first twentieth-century generation of Anglo-Welsh writers. Glyn Jones, in his story 'The Water-Music' (which is autobiographical in form) refers to "our English master, who annihilates me with sarcasm when I audibly praise heaven for prose-writers who use two words where one would do", and the preoccupation with the beauty, virility and potential strangeness of *words* which we find also in the work of Dylan Thomas and Gwyn Thomas may well be an echo of an eloquence sensed from another language but no longer understood. Some of this, of course, had slopped over into a much less literary English at no great distance from the writer's ear: a street-corner wit, a rhetoric of verbal rebellion, was characteristic of the ex-Welsh industrial society in South Wales during the Depression of the twenties and thirties, the time when many of these writers were at the formative stage.

But we have run before our horse to market. The causes of the great burst of twentieth century Anglo-Welsh writing are plain enough, if its features are more arguable. What is so odd is that effect took two extra decades to follow cause. If we take 1915 as a reasonable date for the beginning of a new era (not merely because of the

49. 'Unemployed Miners'. Watercolour by M. Sochachewsky, 1937

publication of *My People*, which will be referred to presently, but because the earliest products of the new County Schools should have been bringing their literary wares to editors and publishers by then) we are faced with the surprising fact that it was certainly 1937 before any sufficient number of writers appeared together to impress the reading public and to suggest that 'something had happened' in Wales. The causes of this time-lag perhaps concern us only marginally. They may be summarised under two heads – the small size of the County Schools (a future writer like Idris Davies, for instance, chose not to enter one) and the restrictively academic nature of their curriculum and teaching methods, which emphasised accurate memorisation as the means to examination success (something which kept potential writers, amongst others, in a state of arrested development).

It may be observed that the writer of the thirties and forties was usually a late developer: Dylan Thomas was an exception because he 'bucked' the system from the outset with the single-minded intention to become a poet, and Alun Lewis another because he was taught English at Cowbridge Grammar School, a school of English mould, by an Englishman. The restrictive academicism of the County Schools may also have been one reason why Idris Davies, alone of Anglo-Welsh poets, was able to tackle directly the bitter realities of the General Strike of 1926 and the years of deprivation in the Valleys. Others, little different in social origin, were either silent except for what Gwyn Thomas has called "a sidling malicious obliquity" or took refuge in rural values which their education had allowed them to approve.

Causes which were fully operative, then, from 1905 or thereabouts did not produce

50. Ernest Rhys at eighty. Frontispiece to
Wales England Wed

generally noticeable effects until 1937. And between these dates, despite the outrunners whom we shall describe, the older type of writing continued. It is impossible, for example, to see Ernest Rhys (1859-1962), Arthur Machen (1863-1947) or W.H. Davies (1871-1940), despite their long writing careers, as having much in common with the new dispensation. Or, for that matter, Edward Thomas (1878-1917), with his much shorter one. Rhys, born in Islington but brought up for a few years in Carmarthen, the son of a runaway marriage between a Welsh Divinity student and a Yorkshire girl, has been of recent years too readily written off, because of his considerable labours as an editor and an anthologist, as a mere bookman. His autobiography, *Wales England Wed* (1940), makes plain, of course, his involvement in the London scene, but in *Welsh Ballads* (1898) his handling of Welsh themes in verse has a directness and an absence of self-conscious apology much more attractive than some of the comparable enterprises of Lewis Morris. And where he deals with more contemporary subjects, as he does in 'The Ballad of the Homing Man', he can accommodate both the commuter-observer and the need for train-rock in the verse:

> He saw above the sallows the first lamps, lemon-hued,
> Lead out the painted suburb into the hazel wood.
>
> He saw the bob-tailed rabbits above the stoneman's pit
> Where the years went, as the trains go, all unawares of it.

It is time that he received the greater due his quality deserves.

Arthur Machen, too, became involved in the London book scene, though less steadily and with less financial success. Brought up at Llanddewi Rectory within sight of Twyn Barlwm and the long ridge of Mynydd Maen in Gwent, he was educated at Hereford Cathedral School and went to London, ostensibly as a medical student. Easily deterred from his studies by his feebleness in mathematics, he endured a period of garret-starvation before making his way as a translator of some distinction (his *The*

51. Arthur Machen, translator, writer and actor, in the Roman amphitheatre at Caerleon, 1937

Heptameron and *The Memoirs of Jacques Casanova* are still thought of by many critics as the best). But ultimately his reputation rests on his stories – if we leave on one side the fortuitous mythological success of 'The Bowmen' (1915) – in which the Gwent countryside of his youth is the focal enchantment within which his love of the occult could bloom. 'The Shining Pyramid', 'The Children of the Pool' and 'The Terror' are the most readily discernible branches of an unusual tree.

In unusualness, however, William Henry Davies yielded to no writer. Born in Pillgwenlly, a dockside village long since part of Newport, of a Welsh mother and a father who, dying early, left the boy's West Country grandparents as the chief influence on his childhood, he developed at school an enthusiasm for poetry which was afterwards suppressed by apprenticeship to a picture-frame-maker and departure, penniless, for London and America. *The Autobiography of a Super-Tramp* (1908) – the author having lost a foot jumping the trains in Canada – was the beginning of a slow movement from London doss-houses (at which stage he was first helped by Edward Thomas and others) to a later life of married respectability at Nailsworth. W.H.Davies wrote no fewer than 749 poems, almost all of them short lyrics: his field of literary reference was entirely English and severance from his birthplace (very occasional visits apart) accentuated the strange limbo in which he wrote – only a persisting simplicity, a sharpness of observation and an occasionally disquieting vision resisting the datedness of the influences that had shaped him. At any branching of the Anglo-Welsh tree he would have been 'a sport', unclassifiable except by extending the catalogue. In addition to several other prose works, Davies also wrote what he was pleased to call an opera – *True Travellers* (1923).

52. Alderman Mrs. Hart shaking hands with W.H. Davies at Newport, 1930

Of the writers of the interim period we are describing, Edward Thomas is much the most important. The son of London Welsh parents, he passed his childhood at various South London addresses and went to school at St. Paul's. Already writing nature articles before he went to university, he read History at Lincoln College, Oxford, under Owen M. Edwards, married Helen Noble, daughter of the critic who had first encouraged him towards a literary career, and began work at once as a full-time writer and reviewer (in which he was by no means, despite his often reiterated anxieties, unsuccessful financially). Often subject to severe bouts of depression, Thomas worked hard and concentratedly: his published books of essays, criticism, nature and topography number more than twenty for the short sixteen or so years of his unimpeded writing life – amongst them *Beautiful Wales* (1905), *The Heart of England* (1906) and *Rose Acre Papers* (1910). He also wrote a novel called *The Happy-Go-Lucky Morgans* (1913), edited John Dyer's poems (1903) and *Celtic Stories* (1911), and kept in touch with Wales by regular visits to Swansea and to Pontarddulais where his cousins and his friend *Gwili* lived. He was even, for a disastrous few months in 1908,

53. Corporal Edward Thomas, Artists' Rifles,
April 1916

Assistant Secretary to The Royal Commission on Welsh Monuments. But he lived always in the countryside of southern England, mainly at Steep in Hampshire, and at the heart of much of his writing was an ingrained sadness at the passing of the traditional way of life in the country, at the gradual break-up of the rural community with the arrival of machines on the farm, quicker communications and increasing urbanisation. Edward Thomas's reputation now rests, however – and it may be subject to change when his prose is carefully reassessed – on the poetry he wrote as Edward Eastaway in the last twenty months of his life, after he had enlisted in the Artists' Rifles. Published for the most part posthumously, his poems are steeped in the melancholy of the changing countryside: they are poems of memory and acceptance, of an unswerving honesty, of an unwillingness to stop at appearances – even when the rhythm of conversation in the verse (of which Thomas is technically a pioneer), its platitudes and omissions, suggests submersion in the norm. "I cannot like the scent", he wrote in 'Old Man',

> Yet I would rather give up others more sweet,
> With no meaning, than this bitter one.

It is an attitude which more and more poets have come to respect in the years that have followed Thomas's death at Arras at Easter 1917. There can be few writers who have been so influential two and three generations on.

XII 'The First Flowering'

The choice of any precise date as marking the beginning of a new period – and 1915 is no exception – is inevitably subject to a good deal of hedging. The reasons for choosing such a date will be underlined presently. But it cannot be denied that for many writers (if few of importance) the spirit of the nineteenth century was projected, with only very gradual change, into the twenties and even the thirties of the twentieth. This can be best illustrated, perhaps, from the anthologies of the period. The earliest so far traced is one called *The Poetry of Wales*, edited by John Jenkins and published at Llanidloes in 1873. It purports to be a volume of translations from Welsh poets made by various hands, including the editor's. There are also four poems in English on Welsh subjects by Felicia Hemans and twenty-one such unacknowledged, presumably the work of the editor himself. The anthology may, of course, have been a device to get John Jenkins's work before the public, but if it is a genuine response to the increasing needs of English-speakers, then its ignorance of Anglo-Welsh writing (including the work of Vaughan and Dyer) is a severe comment on the weakness of that tradition. Edmund O. Jones's *Welsh Lyrics of the Nineteenth Century* (1896), again a product of Llanidloes, honestly embodies its title: it is a book of translations from the Welsh made by the editor. Thus far the spirit of Wales is displayed as originating and still existing, almost exclusively, in the Welsh language. There was, as has been shown, no group of writers in English inside Wales with the cohesion or the confidence to suggest or support an anthology.

Outside Wales one such project came to fruition, though in a pan-Celtic context. Elizabeth Sharp's *Lyra Celtica* (1896), however, devoted only sixteen of its 372 pages to the Anglo-Welsh. The five poets who occupied this space were George Meredith, Sebastian Evans, Ebenezer Jones, Emily Davis and Ernest Rhys – none of them, so far as is known, resident in Wales. Another sixteen pages, earlier in the book's chronology, were given over to translations from Llywarch Hen, Aneirin, Taliesin, Dafydd ap Gwilym and Rhys Goch.

The appearance in 1917, therefore, of an anthology entitled *Welsh Poets* and consisting entirely of original poems in English, undoubtedly marks a stage of advance. But close scrutiny of this collection reveals that the only contributors who show themselves as Anglo-Welsh in either of the later meanings of the term are the editor, A.G. Prys-Jones, Ernest Rhys, Wilma Buckley and Ellen Lloyd-Williams. Pale and barely recognisable as Welsh either in matter or manner, most of the poems in this anthology demonstrate only too clearly how small the advance had been amongst English-speakers, inside Wales or out of it. It was wartime, of course, and Prys-Jones, now the doyen of Anglo-Welsh writers, is very much on his own in showing a *Welsh* spirit as distinct from a vaguely Romantic one: W.H. Davies's offering is undistinguished, and the only other contributors whose literary quality is worthy of mention are Oliver Davies, son of a builder from Llechryd, who was a prison officer at Dartmoor and Stafford, and the Hon. Evan Morgan, later Lord Tredegar, who was to publish *At Dawn* (1924), *The Eel and Other Poems* (1926) and *The City of Canals* (1929) without increasing his reputation. Oliver Davies had already (before *Welsh Poets*) published a volume of frail and musical short-lined lyrics in *Songs at Random* (1912), and was to publish several more.

Welsh Poets was a marker, then, but more important for Prys-Jones's stance as editor than for the feeling of the anthology itself. It was to be a long time yet to

54. A.G. Prys-Jones in 1917

Keidrych Rhys's wartime anthology *Modern Welsh Poetry* (1944) – a sadly misleading title. That was the product of a new generation and a new confidence.

Outside and beyond anthologies, too, writing in prose and poetry continued to blur any impression of definitive change. Promising new writers were beginning to appear – Dorothy Edwards, for instance, whose *Rhapsody* (1927) Arnold Bennett thought revealed "a subtle and intriguing talent" – but they were largely masked by the increasing press of popular novelists – lke Ellis Lloyd (*Scarlet Nest*, 1919, and *A Master of Dreams*, 1921) – most of whom were trying to do for other areas of Wales what Allen Raine had done for Cardiganshire. Of all these intermediaries perhaps only Joseph Keating (1871-1934), with his realistic descriptions of work in the pits – in *Son of Judith* (1900), *Maurice* (1905) and *Flower of the Dark* (1917) – pointed towards new development, though even these works were stagey and, as Glyn Tegai Hughes puts it, "cold fictions, novelistic graftings onto reality".

The twenties and early thirties changed popular attitudes only very slowly. Hindsight, of course, can describe them as a time of little-noticed beginnings – of Richard Hughes, not then associated with Wales, in his first bursts of precocity, of Glyn Jones, with a few poems published in *The Dublin Magazine*, of Geraint Goodwin, trying his hand at the novel with *Call Back Yesterday* (1934), of Jack Jones with *his* first novel *Rhondda Roundabout* (1934), of the few Welsh contributions that Robert Herring made a place for in *Life and Letters*. But the period, seen more realistically, shows old and new confused. The old is well exemplified in the verse of Huw Menai. Originally from Gwynedd but at the relevant time a weigher at a pit in Gilfach Goch, Huw published *Through the Upcast Shaft* in 1920: but as a poet he had washed off the coal-dust only too thoroughly. Over-influenced by Wordsworth, he is persistently sententious: his work appears to the modern reader that of a far more verbose W.H. Davies without the ability to shape and clinch. Here and there a poem almost succeeds, like 'To One Who Died in a Garret in Cardiff' –

55. Huw Menai (Huw Menai Williams) at home in
     Penygraig, Rhondda

No more to quote Mynyddog, or the wise
Khayyam, around the cup . . . .
Asleep beneath the Odes of Arvon skies,
The wine all frozen up . . . .

– but his later collections, down to *The Simple Vision* (1945), show no significant advance.

Newer – and part of a deliberate attempt to strike a positive attitude – were the competent and 'popular' post-Georgian verses of E.Howard Harris and Melfin W. Jones. Harris's *Songs in Shot Silk* (1924) and *Singing Seas* (1926) have an air of direct response to the lead given by A.G. Prys-Jones, whose own *Poems of Wales*, rhythmic and memorable, had been published in 1923. With Melfin Jones's *The Dial Hand* (1932) and *The Hour Glass* (1936), they echo the new and more patriotic sound, the first response in English from Swansea and the Vale of Glamorgan. It was the way in which the popular tradition, if still unrepresentative, could be expected to develop – provided there were no literary undertow. And by the side of these books of verse appeared *First Day* (1935), the earliest collection of Clifford Dyment who, though brought up in Caerleon, has never been seen as Anglo-Welsh, largely because his subsequent and very reputable writing appeared to have no roots in Wales. These were the contrasts, then – tug and counter-tug, advance and retard. It was all piecemeal.

It is because we can discern one new and coherent attitude growing amongst some writers – writers who came into their own from 1937 onwards – that the date 1915 is suggested for the emergence of *modern* Anglo-Welsh writing – *modern* in the sense that it was the product of the new linguistic, social and educational situation already outlined and *modern*, too, in the sharpness and confidence with which it treated the matter of Welshness. The last few pages have made plain the lack of any general (rather than local) direction in the development of Anglo-Welsh writing after 1900 and (despite the honourable persistence of *The Welsh Outlook*) the absence of any focal

56. Caradoc Evans. Caricature by Matt

point of publication – such a magazine as *Wales* became from 1937 onwards. It was in the midst of this flux that a maverick Welsh-speaker in the person of Caradoc Evans (1878-1945) supplied the definition that few of the Welsh public wanted then but that many writers were to take note of later. Caradoc, with his savagely distorted Biblical style, his concentration on greed, lust and hypocrisy, his steadfast omission of compensating virtue, his limitation of subject – all based, as he put it, on the Book of Genesis and Marie Lloyd – had been led by *Draig Glas* and his nose for the market to see where his grudge-writing might be made to pay. Bitterly resenting both his immediate family's fall in status and reputation in the Cardiganshire village of his boyhood and the slavery of his days in the drapery trade, he determined to sell to a London readership some of the Neanderthal activities he could evoke no more than a few hours' journey from the exquisite civilisation of the metropolis. The weakness of his later work (as well as his earliest) reveals to what an extent his best writing depended on the emotional drive of hatred: but by trial and error he perfected a method which, in the short story, is disturbingly effective. His Cardiganshire peasants, darkened with a few strokes, still shock even the jaded reader. *My People* and *Capel Sion*, published in 1915 and 1916 respectively, are those books in which the passion and the talent serve each other best.

Caradoc's chief importance here is that he showed what could be done with the Welsh heritage by a twentieth century writer in English. If what could be done was to 'sell it', nobody can deny that the period of the First World War and its aftermath was a time when the Welsh language was losing ground rapidly, when 'enlightenment' was understood as meaning the abandonment of a peasant past. It is also true that the successful education of the majority of Welsh people by way of the Nonconformist Sunday Schools had brought up generations familiar with religious and political principles but largely ignorant of the culture in the Welsh language which until the eighteenth century had been cherished by the few. When the religious motive weakened and the political was seen to be more potent in English, no great pressure, except in rural areas, was needed to hasten the move away from the Welsh language already prompted by English immigration into south-east Wales. In other words, a high degree of negligence towards the values of Welsh society as it had existed in the nineteenth century was characteristic of many Welsh-speakers, and Caradoc, one of whose targets was 'Modernism' in Welsh Nonconformity (for he was essentially a sidelines conservative in this respect) was surprised that his work produced such an uproar. Surprised but not displeased. He had sold *My People* to Andrew Melrose the publisher on the basis that what he had written was *true*, an *exposé* in strictly descriptive terms of the sub-human characteristics of the Welsh peasant, and he determined to keep the pot boiling by a continual correspondence in the press to confirm it. If it looked like dying out, he always started it up again. When his play *Taffy* was shouted down by London Welshmen in 1923 he was confident that his reputation was assured.

No other Anglo-Welsh prose writer in the succession displayed such ill-will to Wales or to Welsh people, but there is no doubt that a direction had been indicated: in one way or another success in the London market (and it had to be the London market for writers in English) was to be achieved by exploiting the differences and the peculiarities of what many had come to think of as a backward and confined way of life in Wales, a life dominated by chapel pieties and disciplines (many of them observed, as La Rochefoucauld once defined it, only with the homage that vice pays to virtue), by trade union conformities and by the tyrannies of an examination-ridden educational ladder that appeared the only certain way out. The writing of the post-Caradoc phase was done, too, against a background of severe industrial depression: and the reaction of the 'mongrel' society, then at a still lively stage of the mix, was often one of witty hyperbole, of the sort that a writer with a good ear could develop. It is not unfair to

57. Rhys Davies: the young writer in London, about 1932

comment, with the advantage of hindsight, that the success of many of those in the first wave of *modern* Anglo-Welsh writers was based as much on the novelty of their material and their approach to it as on their innate literary ability. To re-read the early numbers of *Wales*, which created a verbal *furore* between 1937 and 1940, is to realise that those who still talk of a 'golden era' then are misled by a temporary *English market* judgement, which a longer perspective cannot possibly support. The London appetite for Welsh eccentricities – not to mention the eccentricities themselves – has died long since.

But market success there undoubtedly was, and for no mere moment. The first short-story writer to capitalise on Welsh eccentricities was Rhys Davies, whose first book, *The Withered Root*, was published in 1927. Born in the Rhondda Valley, Davies went to London before he was out of his teens and learned his craft the hard way. His early writing, however, which was exclusively about Wales, was probably less affected by Caradoc Evans and his success than by the work of D.H. Lawrence, who had exploited the peculiarities of his own Notts-Derby coalfield society in a manner likely to engage those who themselves had mining townships to describe. In dealing with rural society and periods before his own, Davies nevertheless revealed himself – even as late as *The Black Venus* (1944) – heir to the florid Romanticism of much earlier writing. Later, however, in a long literary career, Davies moved on to writing about France and a subject matter more consistent with his continued residence in London and abroad which is distinguished by a spare neutrality in the narration and the suppression of values other than the aesthetic. But it is noticeable that, even in a volume as late as *The Darling of Her Heart* (1958), the Welsh short story is still imprisoned, for him, in three or four attitudes that were laid down by about 1930.

Absence from Wales dictated this, of course, and Glyn Jones, the next writer to appear, has by continuous residence, moved more with the times. But the early stories of this gifted Merthyr man, poet first and then prose-writer, demonstrate much less interest in run-of-the-mill observation of an industrial 'Valley' society than in choosing extraordinary, sometimes supernatural, situations, and emphasising peculiarities. In part the short-story form presses the writer in this direction, but it is also true that Glyn Jones set his signature to prose lyrics of which the motivation was often to describe characters who were physically or sartorially peculiar. *The Blue Bed*, published in 1937, and *The Water Music* (1944), established a reputation that he would perhaps rather have sought as a poet.

For as a poet he was – and still is – conspicuously a 'word-man' (if behind that can be discerned a suffering as well as a beautiful world), and in this his link with Dylan Thomas and others is plain. Lyricism could absorb regret or tragedy just as it could joy, and the 'direction' so far discussed for the post-Caradoc age was subordinated in poetry to the dazzle of words. Some of the reasons for this have already been indicated. In the case of Dylan Thomas (1914-53), however, the influence of Gerard Manley Hopkins must not be forgotten, particularly in the sense that the Welsh prosody in which the latter had experimented put a premium on word- and phrase-intricacy and inventiveness at the possible expense of overall meaning and message. From this same source may have come Dylan Thomas's instinctive requirement of a tight discipline in poetry, the preference (as Vernon Watkins put it) for playing tennis with two nets rather than one.

Nevertheless (to return to 'direction' for a moment), Dylan Thomas demonstrated

58. Vernon Watkins, John Prichard, Alfred Janes, Daniel Jones and Dylan Thomas: a BBC broadcast from Swansea, 1947 (John Griffiths, producer, standing)

two aspects of the alienation that had already taken place amongst the Anglo-Welsh as a result of the social and educational attitudes prevalent since the beginning of the century, two aspects that are inter-related: a dislike, even a hatred, of Welsh-speaking Wales and his ancestry in it (though this was to change after he had been to London) and a completely English field of literary reference. The singleness of mind with which he desired to be a poet and his intention above all to *get to* London, where, his Romantic history of poetry told him, poets lived and worked and were intellectually fed, both speak further of his alienation from the Welsh attitude of the poet as part of his community. All this was to be gravely modified in time, and the achievement of Dylan Thomas, most of all in changing the direction of *English* poetry for at least fifteen years, is not, of course, to be contained within a formula of this sort. Nevertheless, the Romantic isolation and the loss of community were never remedied or undone: even in Dylan's later poetry – and in the stories which must stand with it as his supreme achievement – the Wales we find is the Wales of a child or an adolescent, in all respects save that of landscape with its non-human inhabitants and the cloud of inevitable mortality.

Other poets who appeared in the magazine *Wales*, like Idris Davies (1905-53), showed the same tendency to deride a way of life which, later, they were bitterly to regret when they saw it vanishing. In his case the applied aestheticism sat rather oddly

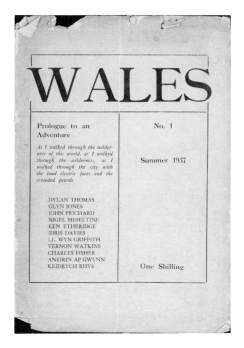

59. *Wales.* Cover of the first number, 1937

upon the moral indignation with which he treated the economic tragedy of his country. And Keidrych Rhys, the magazine's editor, plainly intended, despite some lip-service to the spirit of community and its part-time literary tradition, to rid Wales of its backward eccentricities as quickly as possible and to demonstrate, rather as Henry Vaughan had sought to do three centuries earlier, that there was culture, vitality and talent west of Severn sufficient to compete successfully on *English* terms.

Wales's first issue in 1937 – though a *mélange* of writers old and new – certainly warned London that the Anglo-Welsh had arrived. If, to strictly contemporary palates, its contents seem intrinsically frothy and astringent rather than positive and well-mixed, that may be because the whole scene is different now and values are different too. Two of the poets to be found in it – Lynette Roberts and Ken Etheridge (1911-1981) – though they had subsequent volumes published (Lynette's *Poems* appeared in 1944 and her *Gods with Stainless Ears* in 1951 and Ken's *Songs of Courage* in 1940 and *Poems of a Decade* in 1958) were to desert poetry for long periods; Nigel Heseltine, whose *Tales of the Squirearchy* (1946) struck a new note in Anglo-Welsh prose writing and who was one of *Wales*'s early editors, disappeared overseas and wrote nothing else; and of the three or four writers of ultimate importance involved in the new magazine one at least – the poet Vernon Watkins (1906-67) – was not at all interested in the issues as seen by Keidrych Rhys. But what confirmed an English public in their belief that they were encountering the very stuff of Welshness was the impact in prose of an exaggeratedly different world peopled by characters to whom words – words lyrical, witty, ingenious, poured into new connotations – were the proudest part of living. How often does a new magazine open with such 'nerve' and impact as this?:

As I walked through the wilderness of this world, as I walked through the wilderness, as I walked through the city with the loud electric faces and the crowded petrols of the wind dazzling and drowning me that winter night before the West died, I remembered the winds of the high, white world that bore me and the faces of a noiseless million in the busyhood of heaven staring on the afterbirth.

This passage (the author, of course, was Dylan Thomas) has the confidence to call up echoes of Bunyan and at the same time to mark its style with an individuality born of later crisis.

And the poetry? Insofar as this, too, was carried by the soaring reputation of Dylan Thomas – long past his first appearances in *The Sunday Referee* and with *18 Poems* (1934) and *Twenty-Five Poems* (1936) already published – the tone was no less heady. Dylan used a frequently Biblical vocabulary and applied it to a curious and apparently sexual subject matter, touching the whole off with a kind of affirmatory, preaching zeal which, if too rarely based on discernible argument, was a sub-conscious recollection of the *hwyl* of the Nonconformist preacher in a discarded rural past. He was the Joyce of Wales, unfrocked minister to his unfrocked priest.

Idris Davies's degree of alienation was largely a response to the attitude he found amongst his poet contemporaries. Rhymney-born, familiar with spoken Welsh but lacking a secondary education, he chose the simpler poetic structures available in English and his political commitment led him towards the bitterness of his earlier poems about the Valley communities which were published in *Gwalia Deserta* (1938) and *The Angry Summer* (1943). His work, though too often flawed and simplistic, was unique in attempting to treat the staring injustice of the industrial situation directly

60. Dylan Thomas. Portrait by Alfred Janes   61. Idris Davies

and he was one of the few who used, with more than occasional success, the speech rhythms of his native community.

> Man alive, what a belly you've got

is the mark of a colloquialism that introduces more successful poems than the threadbare, would-be literariness of

> Do you remember 1926? The great dream and the swift disaster,
> The fanatic and the traitor, and more than all,
> The bravery of the simple, faithful folk?

Later, when he had become a teacher in London and had mingled sufficiently with other poets, he became more self-consciously aesthetic. 'Sonnet' in the first issue of *Wales* begins:

> I tossed my golden anchor to the sea
> To tease the twisted tides of salty joy . . .

And with this appeared, too, a disillusion with his former passion and with the past values of his native community. It was a superficial alienation which his short life had barely time to rectify.

62. Jack Jones, handing over the manuscript of his short stories about Merthyr for publication, March 1966. Glyn Jones is on his left

63. Gwyn Thomas: a Christmas greeting to
Glyn Jones, 1949

In the wake of this outward-running wave went supporting combers. There were, for example, the novels and short stories of Gwyn Thomas (1913-81), beginning belatedly with *The Dark Philosophers* (1946) and *The Alone to the Alone* (1947). Here again the emphasis on words, on the dexterities of wit and ribald or rebellious conversation, reflected both the economic desperation and the extraordinary social 'mix' of the South Wales Valleys in the years of the Depression. But unlike Lewis Jones (1897-1939), the leader of the hunger marchers, whose novels *Cwmardy* (1937) and *We Live* (1939) were somewhat wooden attempts to depict 'working-class history' – unlike, too, Jack Jones (1884-1970), of whose many novels *Bidden to the Feast* (1938) and *Off to Philadelphia in the Morning* (1947) were perhaps the most popular, novels in which the liveliness of action, the sense of life lived in the mass and an adequate order of historical events have to compensate for inadequate characterisation and a good deal of cliché writing – Gwyn Thomas offers, in five of his earlier novels particularly, a portrait of a hostile and impenetrable world in which even his Existentialist anti-heroes, though endlessly inventive verbally, are ineffective and absurd. What they project is grandiloquence against the undefeatable. This was new material, it is true, and part of its impact lay in that novelty. But Thomas's indignant Socialism held that this was not a *Welsh* situation at all, except by accident of geography: Welsh natives and English immigrants, side by side, were deprived and assaulted by the indignities of industrial living.

When we meet Bodvan Hemlock, Teilo Thadwald, Denzil Dummock or Shadrach Sims in Gwyn Thomas's pages we are being offered these names and many others as symbols of that hybridity. But Wales is not being 'sold' in these terms, comically or otherwise: the implication is clear that 'the Welsh' have no more to market than any

64. A still from *How Green Was My Valley*, directed by John Ford, 1941

other downtrodden proletariate which has lost all ethnic particularity: the writing has European, Absurdist overtones. It was perhaps the change of feeling in Welsh society since *A Frost on my Frolic* (1953) which made this kind of projection difficult for Gwyn Thomas to repeat.

Other contemporary novelists, in any case, began from positions very different. If we omit Howard Spring, who, though born in Cardiff (a fact which he celebrated in *Heaven Lies About Us* (1939), had made his great popular successes – *O Absalom* (1938) and *Fame is the Spur* (1940) – of Manchester material, it may be true to say that many of them, so far from agreeing with Gwyn Thomas, had moved back to a pre-Caradoc position, in which 'Welshness' was something to celebrate. The difference between the writing of 1945 and that of 1910 was, of course, in the new confidence, in the consciousness of the English audience there waiting, in the knowledge that the 'strangeness' of Wales was very far from exhausted. The most remarkable market success in this genre was Richard Llewellyn's *How Green Was My Valley* (1939), in which the myth of a pure and uncontaminated Welsh society – a society of pioneers (comparable with that in Owen Wister's *The Virginian* and many another such) – is gradually degraded by the arrival of greater numbers, by immigrant blood, by industrialisation and a failure of ideals. The grimy economic and psychological consequences of it all are symbolised in the great tip which overhangs the narrator's house and drives him, like the other surviving members of his family, away from the valley. The novel was an exercise in Romanticism which the English, themselves in a late stage of industrialisation, found especially poignant and the more believable, in

65. Hilda Vaughan and daughter Shirley at Builth Wells, 1936

the irrelevant terms of history, because it took place in a society with which they were still only very partially acquainted. A strong emotional charge in the author – a sense of Welshness lost – helped to produce a success which, in the many novels he wrote afterwards, he found it hard to equal.

A more rural Romanticism was provided by Hilda Vaughan, Michael Gareth Llewelyn and Richard Vaughan, though their regions, all in South Wales, were a little separated geographically. Hilda Vaughan's long career as a novelist had begun as early as 1925 with the publication of *The Battle to the Weak* and her stories of the Radnorshire/ Breconshire/ Herefordshire border, didactic as well as sentimental, were well-plotted and intensely readable. Her work was often – as, for instance, in *The Soldier and the Gentlewoman* (1932) – a somewhat ironic resuscitation of the spirit of Allen Raine, with the greater class-consciousness of the anglicised border counties properly realised and the characters more firmly drawn. For Michael Gareth Llewelyn the scene was either the Vale of Glamorgan or one of the more westerly mining valleys. Perhaps his most successful novel was *White Wheat* (1947), the re-creation of the tale of Wil Hopcyn and the Maid of Cefn Ydfa. With Richard Vaughan there was a move further west still and north, to the flanks of the Carmarthenshire Bannau around Llanddeusant: *Moulded in Earth* (1951), the first of several very successful novels, took another necessary step – backwards in history: the life and times of the farming community are, in the result, enlarged and vitalised beyond the reader's memory or power of self-identification. It is an exercise in the obscurely heroic. The still more recent novels of Alexander Cordell – *Rape of the Fair Country* (1959) and its several

66. T. Harri Jones in Australia, *c.* 1960

successors – though sited in the industrial valleys, belong to the same tradition. Cordell, an Englishman long resident in Wales, makes his history identifiable and gets most of what he needs of it right: but the characters in Garndyrus or amongst the hosts of Rebecca are, if protagonists central to the narrative, not less than ten feet tall. What books in this genre offer is an Anglo-Welsh version of 'the frontier', the American dream ferried home again.

It may appear that the writings of Gwyn Thomas and those of Richard Llewellyn, Cordell and others have little in common. There are, of course, several senses in which this appearance is no less than truth. But it should be remembered that they are all at one in the idiosyncratic use of language and in their need to look outward – whether towards an emerging international ideology or, more simply, towards a market outside Wales. They were undertaken, more obviously as to the later rather than the earlier, in the afterglow of the *furore* which the impact of a supposed Welshness had created in London. The spread of the sociological myth – supported by the 'instant' and rabelaisian Dylan of the pubs – created the feeling for a number of years after 1953 (amongst those classes not affected by the 'dislike' of Welshmen during the Depression) that anything sufficiently verbose and outgoing that could call itself Welsh had a claim to attention.

Perhaps this is the place to discuss briefly the work of another poet, T. Harri Jones (1921-65), who, though later in appearance, was initially influenced by Dylan Thomas and wrote, in part, out of a more enduring love-hate relationship with Wales than had moved his mentor. A native of Llanafan in North Breconshire and a boy from one of the poorer families in an impoverished district, Harri Jones, after taking first-class honours in English at Aberystwyth, worked his way at length into an academic post – but in Newcastle, Australia. His poetry took a long time to rid itself of too-obvious literary influences, but the deeply-felt treachery to the hardness of his ancestors in accepting the softness and perpetual sun of the Antipodes, the failure of sex as a substitute for religion, and the knowledge that the Wales he hated and longed for no longer existed made his last two collections, *The Beast at the Door* (1963) and *The Colour of Cockcrowing* (1966) memorable and affecting to read. His poem 'Back?' ends in this way:

> Of course I'd go back if somebody'd pay me
> To live in my own country
> Like a bloody Englishman.
>
> But for now, lacking the money,
> I must be content with the curlew's cry
> And the salmon's taut belly
>
> And the waves, of water and of fern
> And words, that beat unendingly
> On the rocks of my mind's country.

XIII 'The First Flowering': Other Voices

To have pointed out a certain direction in much of the writing done from 1915 onwards is not at all the same thing as being able tidily to associate every writer of significance with that direction. It will be possible presently to show that *some* writers had different objectives altogether. But even that cannot complete the tally. There are a few writers of importance who must be treated outside the main generalisations. Two of these belong to the Welsh border country.

Margiad Evans (1909-58) was no more than a quarter Welsh despite her choice of pseudonym and, since her formative years were spent near Ross-on-Wye, it is not certain how much of her writing about Wales was based on personal experience. But her early books, *Country Dance* (1932) and *The Wooden Doctor* (1933), demonstrate a lyrical sympathy with Welsh tradition and feeling. How this is related to her more intense later works, *Autobiography* (1943) and *Ray of Darkness* (1952), in which the detail of the natural scene and the stress on the inter-connection and unity of the created world enabled her, as Idris Parry has put it, "to immerse her *self* and become a thing among things", is not yet clear.

If, for all her ability to integrate herself, Margiad Evans may still be suspected of being a Romantic outsider, no such thought can possibly be entertained of Geraint Goodwin (1903-41). Separated by birth in Newtown from the *shonihois* of the South, he took the advice of Edward Garnett and left journalism in London to write, first in Hertfordshire and finally in Wales, about the country folk of his youth. Undoubtedly he was writing *for* London and for that reason, equally without doubt, his Welsh

67. Geraint Goodwin: on holiday at Borth, 1934

characters sometimes have a strange, elusive quality. But the strangeness was more than partly due to the time-gap caused by his use creatively of his mother's recollections of the countryside at the turn of the century: the characters that emerge are worthier than a demand for Welsh eccentricity would have made them: they are often tragic, folk destined to suffer. Goodwin's gifts were considerable: a rapid, often a careless, writer, he had an almost faultless ear for conversation: his feeling for the shape and the necessary omissions of the short story rarely erred: and his deeply human developments of male-female relationships, most of them unsatisfactory, are Lawrentian only superficially – if Lawrence was ever an influence he disappeared from the later writing. Novels came less easily: the much-admired *The Heyday in the Blood* (1936) can be seen as a loosely-grouped collection of stories, but the increasing grasp of *Watch for the Morning* (1938) and *Come Michaelmas* (1939) make Goodwin's early death from tuberculosis a tragedy for Wales's showing in the novel in English.

There are also two poets of high repute who, while belonging to the first period of twentieth century Anglo-Welsh writing (the period which ended, no more than approximately, with the disappearance of the influence of Dylan Thomas) scarcely fit the framework so far constructed for it. What they had in common was an education which removed any need they might have had to join the reaction against the traditional Wales. The first is Vernon Watkins (1906-67), born at Maesteg but brought up in Swansea and Gower. Sent away to preparatory school and then to Repton and Cambridge, he knew very little of the Welsh language or of his family's original Nonconformity: like Dylan Thomas and others, he was a child of 'enlightenment': he was taught to look out and away. But because his formative experience as a poet was unconnected with Wales, he was able to live all his life (except for National Service and visits abroad) in the Gower of his upbringing, taking just so much of Welsh tradition as the driving theme of his poetry needed, without revolt or reconciliation. His personal flowering as one of the few twentieth century metaphysicals was based on the 'grief' he

68. Vernon Watkins. Portrait by Alfred Janes

felt at being wrenched out of a golden youth at Repton into a grim, unpoetic, workaday world (whose grey habit concealed both niggling academicism at Cambridge and the repetitiveness of a bank clerk's existence). Determined to relinquish nothing he had loved or felt, he developed his theme of 'the conquest of time', particularly in his collections *The Lady with the Unicorn* (1948) and *The Death Bell* (1954), into poems of an elusive, cadenced beauty which T.S. Eliot admired and critics applauded without understanding. Linked with Dylan Thomas by friendship and by some of his beliefs about poetry, Watkins was a poetic craftsman of no less skill and even greater labour, who might have been Poet Laureate but for his sudden death at Seattle in 1967. If his use of Welsh tradition was highly selective – only the ancient custom of the Mari Lwyd and the legend of Taliesin (a variant of the latter being associated with his beloved Gower) found a place – the philosophical movement of his poetry from its early involvement with Neo-Platonism towards a still-unorthodox Christianity offers, despite its difficulty, the fascination of a deeply-felt spiritual quest.

The other poet who escapes the net is Alun Lewis (1915-44), born at Cwmaman, Aberdare. He too was a child of 'enlightenment': his upbringing led him away from the Welsh language and family origins in rural Pembrokeshire and Cardiganshire (despite many holidays at Pen-bryn), away, too, from the influence of the Unitarian Chapel towards Socialist idealism and an agnostic, superficially aesthetic, attitude to life. Sent away as a boarder to Cowbridge Grammar School, one of the few schools of English pattern in Wales, he had some precocious success with short stories and learned to set his sights as a writer on London. Despite a brilliant academic career at Aberystwyth and Manchester, he was never in real touch with any contemporary Anglo-Welsh writers (except Lynette Roberts and Brenda Chamberlain) and had left his teaching post at Pengam for the War before he realised (as he did in India, in the last months of his life) that he knew very little of Wales except from the edge of the academic and middle-class cocoon his family had provided for him. War service, during which his

69. Alun Lewis, with his friend Teddy Coles

CASEG BROADSHEET No 1.

Wood Engraving : Debris Searcher.

John Petts.

TWO POEMS *by Alun Lewis*

RAIDERS' DAWN.

Softly the civilised
Centuries fall,
Paper on paper,
Peter on Paul.

And lovers waking
From the night—
Eternity's masters,
Slaves of Time—
Recognise only
The drifting white
Fall of small faces
In pits of lime.

Blue necklace left
On a charred chair
Tells that Beauty
Was startled there.

SONG OF INNOCENCE.

Pyrotechnic shells
From the blackened fair
Break like meteors
In the careless air.

Dancing girls and singing birds,
Poets' and crooners' platitudes
Violently die.

But the simple words
Spoken in shelters, crypts
   and wards
Where the disfigured lie

Are swans in the sky.

Published by the Caseg Press, Llanllechid Caernarvonshire
and printed at the Gomerian Press, Llandyssul, S. Wales.

LLYFRGELL
GENEDLAETHOL
CYMRU

70. Caseg Broadsheet No. 1, 1941

first book of poems, *Raiders' Dawn* (1942), created an immediate stir, took him away from the stylistic influence of Auden, and away, too, from his early aestheticism, uncovering the moral passion which was always part of his poetry. His correspondence with the Bangor-born poet and artist Brenda Chamberlain (whose own collection, *The Green Heart*, was published later, in 1958) illustrates both his early confidence in what art and education could do (particularly in their intention, with John Petts, to create and distribute the Caseg Broadsheets) and India's denial of all such hopes – even that of the changing power of love – within a human time-scale. One of the rare letter-writers of distinction in this century, Alun Lewis achieved much for one who died at twenty-eight: his later poems *Ha! Ha! Among the Trumpets* (published posthumously in 1945), if they confirm an impression that his sensibility was always finer than his control of language, nevertheless show him as a poet of undoubted quality, and his mature stories, particularly 'Ward 03b' and 'The Orange Grove', indicate very clearly what Wales lost by his failure to return.

XIV 'The Second Movement'

That this first twentieth-century wave of Anglo-Welsh writing was deep and rich, far out-topping in its collective foam and grandeur anything that had preceded it, cannot be doubted. But its direction was out and away from Wales. Meanwhile, and often concurrently, a less distinguishable ocean swell (not to be called a wave for a long time yet) was gathering – a movement much less popular, much more erudite, much less immediately successful or desirous of being so, one which, in emphasising heritage and tradition, was already conscious of the damage to the Welsh way of life which so much exploitation and popularisation had caused. It was, in brief, less self-absorbed, reverting to the older Welsh tradition in which the poet had a duty to his community as well as to his muse. According to this tradition the poet was celebrator, commentator, propagandist (under the earlier forms of patronage) and rememberer of the glories and ideals of the past. This spectrum of rights and duties could spread so widely across the poet's sky that the Muse as Ego could be obliterated – or at least be relegated to the occasional gaps in the firmament. David Jones, in his Preface to *The Anathemata* (1952) puts it in this way:

> the workman must be dead to himself while engaged upon the work, otherwise we have that sort of 'self-expression' which is as undesirable in the painter or the writer as in the carpenter, the cantor, the half-back, or the cook. . . .

In other words, the poet has a world to express, a tradition, a meaning, an order: and if few writers would follow David Jones in pressing this so far (even he admitted to finding it difficult in practice), those who belonged to this counter-swell were at one in rejecting exhibitionism, the betrayal of heritage and the primacy of commercial values. Some of them, too, felt it necessary to counter even the more idealistic aspects of the 'outward wave' – Alun Lewis's internationalism, for instance – by emphasising the irreplaceable virtues of 'particularity', of uniqueness and continuity. David Jones's Tribune, in the midst of his equivocal speech on behalf of Empire (*The Tribune's Visitation*, 1958), feels bound to explain one aspect of the relationship between "known-site" and "world-floor":

> As wine of the country
>   sweet if drawn from wood
> near to the living wood
>   that bore the grape
>   sour if taken far
> so can all virtue curdle in transit
> so vice may be virtue uprooted
> so is the honey-root of known-site
>   bitter fruit for world-floor.

In the specific context of Wales there was emphasis on the ancientness of the country's tradition, on the need to hold on to what was left of it in the anglicised areas (something which, of course, Goodwin, Eiluned Lewis and the writers of the never-really-terminated Prys-Jones 'age' could also have claimed) and on using scholarship or belief or both to underline the unique quality of this surviving version of the Celtic community.

These writers of the 'second movement' worked largely in isolation from each other:

71. Glyn Jones, Jack Jones and Gwyn Jones in the house of T. Rowland Hughes, 1948

they were individuals and their only coherence was as Welshmen: they had no magazine outlet like Keidrych Rhys's *Wales*. Yet, while it would be false historically to suggest an antithesis where none certainly existed, there did begin in February 1939 a second literary magazine, *The Welsh Review*, which its editor, Gwyn Jones, developed in a direction more academic and fastidious. Himself a short-story writer and novelist of quality as well as a renowned scholar of the Scandinavian literatures, Gwyn Jones published the work of such diverse contributors as Geraint Goodwin, the then-elderly Caradoc Evans, John Cowper Powys, Margiad Evans and Alun Lewis, besides appearing as the first historian of the development of Anglo-Welsh writing in *The First Forty Years*. Hindsight clearly discerns that the editor of *The Welsh Review* saw the shape and manner of the Welsh contribution to English letters as differing from that apparently appreciated by the market. Yet he himself, with his erudite *Richard Savage* (1935) and his Valleys epic *Times Like These* (1936), his short stories – in *The Buttercup Field* (1945) and later – which straddle the landscape from the industrial to the rural, and perhaps in particular with his evocative translation (with Thomas Jones) of *The Mabinogion* (1948), is that literary figure who of them all is the most difficult to place. His thinking was often that of the first Anglo-Welsh 'movement': but his scholarship and his breadth of interest were all the time making possible its counter.

The earliest work in the second 'movement' (confusingly, it was concurrent with

72. David Jones: *Annunciation in a Welsh Hill Setting, c.* 1963

much that has already been described) was undoubtedly David Jones's *In Parenthesis* (1937), his long-gestated poem (some call it a novel) of the First World War. Although it does no more than hint at the Roman world in which its author, in later poems, was to move so freely, its significance for our present purpose is that the company of Welsh and Cockney soldiers, facing battle together, evokes again, but outside the island, that Matter of Britain which was once the state myth of the Plantagenets and Tudors. The tradition and feeling of the ancient Welsh in the face of the enemy – visible even in that unwarlike friend of the narrator's, Corporal Aneirin Lewis, "who worshipped his ancestors like a Chink" – appears again in an older form than Maurice Kyffin or John Davies of Hereford or James Howell could have given it, overborne as they were by its purely Tudor version. In the later poems of David Jones – except *The Anathemata*, in which he is concerned partly with the validity of the Catholic faith in all ages and partly with the survival of the Matter of Britain up to Tudor times – the order of the Roman Empire is first created and felt, then broken by a special pleading for the rights and contributions of small and cultured peoples, amongst whom the Welsh are plainly closest to the poet's heart. In these later poems the recreated unity of the Island disappears: the positive affirmations of virtue become increasingly associated with the Welsh – a reason, possibly, why the poems are described as 'fragments' of a greater whole (which could never, in David Jones's later attitude of mind, have been completed).

73. Private Jones, 15th Battalion, Royal
    Welsh Fusiliers, 1915

74. Gwyn Williams at Treweithan, Trefenter,
    1969

The enormous erudition displayed in *The Anathemata, The Tutelar of the Place* (1961), *The Hunt* (1965) and *The Sleeping Lord* (1974) – to name only a few of the poems – is linked with an experimental but consistent and idiosyncratic style; together they tend to defeat all but the most serious readers. David Jones is as yet recognised by some critics only, but by them as one of the *great* writers of the twentieth century.

Meanwhile, away in Cyrenaica throughout the forties, Gwyn Williams was translating Welsh verse into English. This had been done before in a limited way – by John Jenkins and Edmund O. Jones, as already recorded, and by H.I. and C.C. Bell in *Welsh Poems of the Twentieth Century in English Verse* (1925) – but the classical heritage of Welsh poetry had been little explored and there was plainly a need to make it accessible in an English open to modern sensibilities. Gwyn Williams's first book of translations, *The Rent That's Due to Love*, appeared in 1950: his *Presenting Welsh Poetry* (1959) initiated, the time being riper, a somewhat wider interest which resulted in the publication of *Mediaeval Welsh Lyrics* (1965) by the American Joseph Clancy (who has since produced several further volumes of translations) and Anthony Conran's *Penguin Book of Welsh Verse* (1967). It is difficult to prove that access to such Welsh sources has markedly influenced Anglo-Welsh poets writing now: perhaps the chief effect has been visible in Conran, whose espousal in his own poetry of the celebratory as well as the elegiac function of Welsh verse has struck an individual note. Gwyn Williams meanwhile – back in Wales first at Trefenter and now at Aberystwyth – has had time to produce, among a number of works, two volumes of his own poetry – *Inns of Love* (1970) and *Foundation Stock* (1974) – as well as another volume of translations from the Welsh, *To Look for a Word* (1976).

Another of the early signs of the 'second movement' excited little attention. In 1946

75. R.S. Thomas at the Sherman Theatre,
     Cardiff, for the celebration of his
     seventieth birthday, 17 May 1983

76. Emyr Humphreys, at Pwllheli, 1952

Keidrych Rhys's Druid Press in Carmarthen published *The Stones of the Field*, a first collection by a then unknown clergyman of the Church in Wales, R.S. Thomas. Seminal in the sense that it contained poems upon subjects that were to occupy many books to follow, *The Stones of the Field* began that love-hate relationship of the priest, lonely in his vocation, with the locationally lonely hill-farmer, which was presently to produce the reconciling *persona* of Iago Prytherch. Disappointment at what he alleged to be venality, ignorance and lack of aesthetic standards did not prevent R.S. Thomas from seeing in his poverty-stricken hill folk (whose prototypes he had found beyond Adda, west of Manafon, his parish in English-speaking Montgomeryshire) the only true Welshmen of a Wales that had been and was still, by one means or another, bitterly oppressed. The George Orwell of Welsh Nationalism had made his entry, only too aware of the fallibility of his countrymen and incapable (in the end) of believing that he or they could deserve the landscape, the veritable soil, of Wales.

Again in 1946 and as little noticed, Emyr Humphreys's first novel, *The Little Kingdom*, was published in London. It was the first presentation in prose of characters with nationalist plans and intentions and its author was plainly not offering his country for outside delectation: the tone is cautionary, moral and pessimistic. The many novels that Humphreys has produced since – and it must not be forgotten that he has also published poetry in *Ancestor Worship* (1970) and short stories in *Natives* (1968) – are not to be labelled undiscriminatingly as 'nationalistic': some of them, like *The Italian Wife* (1957), explore themes that are not Welsh at all. From *A Change of Heart* (1950), and *Hear and Forgive* (1952) (for the latter of which he received the Somerset Maugham Award), he began to develop what he called 'the Protestant novel'

77. Emyr Humphreys producing Saunders Lewis's play, *Brad*, 1958. (l to r) Emyr Humphreys, Emlyn Williams, Siân Phillips, Richard Burton, Hugh David, Gareth Jones, Meredith Edwards and (foreground) Clifford Evans

– or the novel of individual conscience (in itself very much a minority theme in the English society of the fifties). After *A Toy Epic* (1958), written first in Welsh and awarded the Hawthornden Prize on translation into English, then in *Outside the House of Baal* (1965) and the unfinished sextet of novels beginning with *National Winner* (1971) and *Flesh and Blood* (1974), he has concerned himself, on a larger scale and ever more intricately, with the discovery of the pattern of 'good' in society – a pattern which is the link with traditional Wales. When John More in *National Winner* insists to his social climber wife Amy that they are "chapel people all the same" although he hasn't been inside a chapel for "goodness knows how many years" and that he has "philosophical" difficulties about joining the yacht club, Emyr Humphreys is opening up to the reader a much more historical Wales than was ever revealed by the anguished earlier cries of escaping Romantics. His writing is the more challenging, too, for its locale: his frequent, though not inevitable, return to the Flintshire of his birth is one of the signs, now more frequent, that writing in English from Wales is not necessarily an emanation of the Valleys.

It is important to recognise, however, – if we take our stand about the year 1950 – that the individual appearances in which we have been dealing were, without exception, unimpressive in purely commercial terms. It was still the day of the Romantics, of eccentricities and of Dylan's reputation. Many years were to go by yet before David Jones's name was known to more than a few, and Gwyn Williams's work was easily absorbed into the background of scholarly interest appropriate to the university. R.S. Thomas's first book fluttered so few dovecotes in Wales or anywhere else that he was constrained to publish his second, *An Acre of Land* (one of the most stimulating of them all), at his own expense. It is true that by a fortunate accident the radio programme *The Critics*, one of whose participants happened, in the right week in 1952, to be Alan Pryce-Jones, born in the Newtown where *An Acre of Land* was printed, hailed the book as the best volume of poetry seen that year, and R.S. Thomas's reputation was made, in London and hence in Wales. But this was still a recognition of the Heir Apparent and Emyr Humphreys's success during these years, while solidly based enough, was of the kind that left his name almost unknown in Wales outside his own generation at university.

When Dylan Thomas died in New York in 1953 he had already outlived the impetus of the 'first' Anglo-Welsh 'movement'. Idris Davies and Alun Lewis had died before him. Keidrych Rhys's *Wales*, always an enterprise of fits and starts, virtually came to an end in 1949: *The Welsh Review*, probably never a commercial success, had by that same year made altogether too large a hole in its editor's pocket. So much had come to an end and so little was seen to be beginning. The public, never having realised the later Dylan and anxious still to be on 'next round' terms with his earlier *persona*, could think of nothing better to do than mourn and prolong his age by continued acclaim. The succeeding decade was to seem very empty.

Public *support* for Anglo-Welsh writing, however, had never even remotely approached the dimensions suggested by the popular reputation of Dylan Thomas. The failure of *Wales* and *The Welsh Review* proved that an English-language

78. *Dock Leaves*. Cover of first number, December 1949

readership in Wales sufficient for commercial success did not exist, even with the resources of the London Welsh thrown in. Once a wider readership grew less interested – as had to happen when the first emphasis on novelty and eccentricity waned – the cultural poverty of a generation that had already begun to forget the Depression and its stimulus to wit and self-examination became more apparent. The founding of *Dock Leaves* in the far south-west of Pembrokeshire at the end of 1949 does not really cast doubt on this: for *Dock Leaves*, no more commercial than its predecessors, was unorthodoxly supported by the efforts of a coherent group in a small town, willing and able to call on the local patriotism of the unliterary. That it survived and was able, in 1957, to change its name to *The Anglo-Welsh Review* was partly a recognition by its most interested readers that in Wales it stood absolutely alone: it was also partly the result of the ability and vision of its editor, Raymond Garlick, and his consciousness of the new direction being taken by Anglo-Welsh writing.

Nevertheless, *The Anglo-Welsh Review*'s first twelve years were in this respect dispiriting enough, especially in terms of its editor's avowed desire to heal the breach with writers in Welsh that Caradoc Evans had created and the first generation of twentieth-century Anglo-Welsh writers had carelessly allowed to continue, and to move back to a position in which the heritage from Welsh could be conserved and valued. Moreover, the literary scene remained under-populated. Special numbers on

79. Pembroke Dock Literary Group, at Awelon, Manorbier, July 1954: (l to r, standing) Henry Birkhead, Anne Lewis Davies, Raymond Garlick, Morwyth Rees, Roland Mathias, Nora Davies, Albert Coleman: (seated) Eveline Hinchliffe, Jean Bêsida (visitors), Hannah Hughes

Dylan Thomas, David Jones and John Cowper Powys did something to disguise the fact that few, if any, new writers of consequence seemed to be emerging. Outside the *Review*'s pages, of course, established writers continued. Vernon Watkins received increasing applause in London but, despite his many friendships with other poets, was not really aware of a change in the wind. Dannie Abse, who had first been published in the forties, began to move to higher reaches with *Tenants of the House* (1957). But he was by this time cosmopolitan, apparently lost in London. The English-reading public of Wales, largely dependent on London newspapers, followed the wider readership of England in believing that there never had been any Anglo-Welsh writing of importance except from the pen of Dylan Thomas, and he was dead. By hindsight we can now see that during this time the views and attitudes of R.S. Thomas – as expressed in *Poetry for Supper* (1958), *Tares* (1961) and *The Bread of Truth* (1963) – were acquiring a hold over a much more serious and indeed academic sector of the public in Wales than had ever followed Dylan Thomas, and in a much smaller way this was true of Emyr Humphreys too. But it is also important to note that this was so, in the first place, because both were published in London and were held in high esteem there. In this sense it was an interim period. But overt signs of development were so lacking at the time that Raymond Garlick – despite the favourable reception given to his own formally-structured but ingenious and challenging poetry, as seen in *Poems from the Mountain-House* (1950), *The Welsh-Speaking Sea* (1954) and *Blaenau Observed* (1957) – abandoned his editorship of *The Anglo-Welsh Review* at the end of 1960 and took a post in Holland.

XV Growth in the Sixties

Yet, as so often happens, the darkest hour was that just before the dawn. Official subsidy, because literature alone amongst the long-established arts was expected to pay for itself, was at this time manifest only very occasionally, in the form of small deficiency grants. Too late by far to help *Wales* and *The Welsh Review*, these did, if more by good luck than judgement, keep *The Anglo-Welsh Review* going between 1960 and 1963. It was in this latter year that, by a decision taken outside Wales, literature broke out of the mists of the official myth and first qualified positively for public grant. From that point onwards progressively – and especially after the Welsh Committee of the Arts Council of Great Britain was succeeded in 1967 by a Welsh Arts Council with a Literature Department – Anglo-Welsh writers and the journals in which their work appeared became financially able to do whatever it lay in their powers to do. The debt owed to Welsh Arts Council funding in the last eighteen years is incalculably great.

But it may well be doubted whether the burst of new writing that came over the dam in 1964 and 1965 can be related directly to what was then a small improvement in the financial provision. As almost always, a new movement may be traced to active leaders, and if it appeared that the climate was suddenly different, that the clouds had parted, that the sky had a new blue, it was because out of sight a group of writers, not all of them young, had laboured hard in preparation. That the impulse behind the labour was in part nationalistic and in part concerned especially to provide a new platform for the writing of English-speaking Welshmen cannot be denied, nor is there any reason why it should be.

From the autumn of 1962 Meic Stephens and Harri Webb, both then of Merthyr, had corresponded with Bryn Griffiths in London and Tony Conran in Bangor in the hope of stimulating activity amongst Anglo-Welsh writers. The chief result of this was the founding in 1965 of *Poetry Wales*, with Meic Stephens as editor. Meanwhile, in London, where the necessarily few literary pages of *London Welshman*, edited by Tudor David, had been the only element of continuity in the previous decade, Bryn Griffiths had succeeded in gathering round him, in what was a branch of the newly-formed Guild of Welsh Writers, several poets of future reputation in the persons of John Tripp, Sally Roberts (later Sally Roberts Jones), Tom Earley and Robert Morgan. The organisation of this was loose, haphazard: the Guild was perhaps not much more than the declaration in the metropolis of the closer organisation in Cardiff. But the effect, from the moment *Poetry Wales* appeared, was very marked. At once it could be noted that poets like Harri Webb and John Tripp (the latter soon, like Sally Roberts, to be back in Wales) were in rapid production, and that there were others, like John Stuart Williams, Peter Gruffydd, Alun Rees, Robert Morgan, Alison Bielski (one of the very few Anglo-Welsh poets to have experimented widely in verse-forms) and Herbert Williams, who – though few of them were nationalistic in outlook and most had appeared before in the pages of *The Anglo-Welsh Review* – were suddenly more active than they had been. It was one of those sociological air-changes that reflect both a gradual shift of attitude amongst large numbers of academic and professional people and the appearance of the leaders capable of creating and reflecting that shift. The deprived years were over.

The new platform and the new confidence that had brought Harri Webb out of silence had their effect, too, on other poets no longer young. Leslie Norris and John

80. Robert Morgan: leaving the Miners'
    Eisteddfod, Porthcawl, 1949

81. *Poetry Wales*: cover of the first number,
    Spring 1965

82. Leslie Norris: by Trevithick's Tramroad
    in Merthyr Tydfil, 1944

83. John Ormond and Dylan Thomas, June 1946

Ormond, who for personal reasons had published little or nothing for a decade and a half, reappeared, with all the virtues of mature practice. Norris, born in Merthyr Tydfil, had had a Resurgam pamphlet called *The Tongue of Beauty* published in 1943 but had subsequently gone into teaching in England. With the appearance of his Triskel Press pamphlet *The Loud Winter* and his first major collection *Finding Gold* (both 1967) it was clear, not merely that he was still mightily engaged with Wales, and particularly with the Merthyr of memory, but that he had brought to the task a language of poetry both delicately balanced and carefully wrought. John Ormond's case was not entirely dissimilar. Known in Swansea before the War as a poet, he became a film producer and director with the B.B.C. and did not publish his first, long overdue, collection, *Requiem and Celebration*, till 1969. His second volume, *Definition of a Waterfall* (1973), more fully demonstrated both his mature philosophy and his care for poetic structure. In the vein of this book he is a poet very seriously to consider.

Then Dannie Abse, though there had been no such silence from him, had by 1968, with the publication of *A Small Desperation*, consolidated an already strong reputation. Born in Cardiff of Jewish stock, Abse had been a significant figure on the London poetry scene at least since the appearance of his third collection, *Tenants of the House*, in which he had begun to provide for many of his more important poems a symbolic concept or structure which unified the whole and *was* the poem in meaning as well. In his more recent works (such as *Funland*, 1973) this has been replaced altogether by more direct comment (however oblique that directness may sometimes seem). Novelist and dramatist as well as poet, Dannie Abse has published three volumes of autobiography – *Ash on a Young Man's Sleeve* (1954), *A Poet in the Family* (1974) and

84. Dannie Abse reading at Oriel, 1977

A Strong Dose of Myself (1983) – which have been widely read; he is one of the very few Anglo-Welsh writers well known outside Wales. His residence in London, the length of his writing life (his first book was published in 1948) and the wide angle of his poetic viewfinder make of him a bridge figure who is here placed in the 'second movement' partly because his period of recognition is contemporary with it and partly because, though he is certainly no nationalist, the closing of the ranks which has characterised the recent period (to be described presently) has in many respects brought him back to Wales and made his influence felt there.

Meanwhile John Tripp (1927-1986), having abandoned journalism in London specifically to return to Wales, produced several collections – *Diesel to Yesterday* (1966), *The Loss of Ancestry* (1969), *The Province of Belief* (1971) and *The Inheritance File* (1973) – in which he used the fascination of history and a fierce patriotism to weld social comment and polemic. A word-spinner, if occasionally careless of rhythm, his work is rarely less than stimulating to read. It brought immediacy back into poetry, involved a wider public. Immediacy was also the mark of Harri Webb, though his language was very different. One of those who had been silent in his years of precocity, Webb became a librarian and entered politics as a nationalist: his first, too long delayed, volume of poetry, *The Green Desert* – an image he meant for Wales – appeared in 1969. It revealed him uneven as a poet but adept as a balladeer. Some of the poems from the book went onto record: undoubtedly Harri Webb became that poet of all of whom the men of the Valleys had heard. *A Crown for Branwen* (1974), his second book, confirmed that, at his best, he could provide powerful evocations of people and places, and a certain testy vigour informed all that he did. Sally Roberts's *Turning Away* (1969), though quieter, was part of this changed atmosphere: her virtues as a poet were those of sensitivity and reflection within the current feeling. Other books, like John Stuart Williams's *Green Rain* (1967), though they offered directions and emphases rather different, confirmed the new intensity of the literary scene.

85. John Tripp in Whitchurch, Summer 1984

86. Harri Webb at Swansea, 1982, during the shooting of *Memoirs of a Pit Orchestra*, for which he edited the script

87. Cover of *Planet* No. 48. The Referendum of 1979: the Tory elephant on Labour's Aberavon doorstep

Once more there was impetus, the visible creating of a new wave, one for which the older toilers apart had long prepared.

A number of developments followed. First, Welsh writers were reconciled formally to Anglo-Welsh. In 1968 Meic Stephens, who had been appointed, the year previous, Literature Director for the Welsh Arts Council, arranged that the Welsh Academi should receive a deputation of six Anglo-Welsh writers and discuss with them the possibility of forming an English-language Section. Moved by a compelling speech of reconciliation by the veteran Welsh writer D.J. Williams, the Academi accepted the proposition. Second, the range of periodicals supported by Welsh Arts Council subsidy was significantly widened. *Planet*, edited by Ned Thomas from Llangeitho, was founded in 1969 to provide a platform for political and sociological discussion of the problems of Wales, as well as those of minorities everywhere: *Mabon*, edited from North Wales by Alun Jones and Gwyn Thomas (the poet), had as its brief the provision of opportunity for writers still at school: and *Second Aeon*, which was the creation of Peter Finch, developed as an organ of the international poetry scene beloved of younger writers. Third, the new sense of achievement was marked by the appearance of three poetry anthologies, the first since that of Keidrych Rhys in 1944. The earliest of the three was Bryn Griffiths's *Welsh Voices* (1967) which, despite some deficiencies, came to be much used in schools: Gerald Morgan's *This World of Wales* (1968) set out the Anglo-Welsh sequence from the earliest writing and had little space, in consequence, for the contemporary: and *The Lilting House* (1969), compiled by Meic Stephens and John Stuart Williams, besides being the largest, displayed most fully the achievement of the twentieth century. Fourth, and perhaps even more important than the factors already mentioned, a limited number of bursaries was awarded to Anglo-Welsh writers, whose books were also eligible for Welsh Arts Council production grants. Such grants were made, almost exclusively, to Welsh publishers.

The fact that books in English began, from 1968, to be published in Wales in some number was, for the next seven years, to produce a curious boomerang effect: while the Anglo-Welsh writers whose books were published in London remained unaffected, those who elected to publish in Wales found their work, of whatever standard and seriousness, excluded from the review columns of London newspapers and journals – a fate compelled in like manner, if with less success, upon books published in Scotland and the outer regions of England. One of the results of this was that Anglo-Welsh writers became a group more cut off from other writers in English than they had ever been (though they came to know each other the better for it) and were even accused, by one essentially friendly critic, of "talking to themselves".

This in turn, of course, concentrated their readership *in* Wales, and the size and nature of this readership is one of the enduring problems that Anglo-Welsh writers have to face. Briefly, it is still true that, despite the extensive financial patronage of the Welsh Arts Council, a curriculum both at school and university which, for those who do not opt into Welsh, remains, a few institutions excepted, virtually identical with that of England (the cyclical effects of this are very hard to break), a general disregard by the media (newspapers and television in particular) of serious works in English published in Wales, and the difficulties encountered by the majority of Welsh publishers and bookshops (both of them sadly lacking in capital) have combined to leave the English-speaking public of Wales largely uninformed about their own writers and generally of the opinion that they cannot be of any real quality and importance.

Anglo-Welsh poetry and prose were bought, for some years after 1968, far more – and quite disproportionately – by Welsh-speakers whose own journals did provide the necessary information, and only recently, as a result of publicity put out, and events organised, by the English Language Section of the Academi and the more enterprising publishers has this situation begun to change.

Probably these difficulties smack of natural justice to those readers who still think in terms of 'Dylan Thomas dead'. And yet, if the achievement of the Anglo-Welsh in the twentieth century be looked at as a whole, it will be seen that what was so well, if belatedly, begun has just as well continued, if in a different direction. This is the moment, perhaps, at which we should seek to assess the chronological procession thus far.

XVI Further Developments

That almost all writers who emerged before 1900 (and the great majority of those who were published before 1920) may be separated from those who followed on social, professional or geographical criteria is plain enough. Post-War Anglo-Welsh writers spring from a *majority* of the population, not a restricted class or two, and have come, with rare exceptions, through a uniform educational system which may be described as 'English, with a few Welsh-born academic characteristics'. The achievement of those writers who belonged to the earlier dispensation, if we rigorously exclude three of Arthur Quiller-Couch's Metaphysicals – John Donne, George Herbert and Thomas Traherne – and are equally severe with Christopher Smart, George Meredith, William Morris, Wilfred Owen and others who are a generation or two away from the justifiably Anglo-Welsh, is scarcely better than mediocre. Probably only Henry Vaughan, John Dyer, W.H. Davies, Edward Thomas and Arthur Machen set a standard fit for emulation. But from the time of the First World War we are aware of a great upsurge, not always confined within the limits schematically described in these pages. Service with Welsh units in Flanders, for instance, prompted an astonishingly high proportion of the best war writing – and the net here may legitimately draw in Robert Graves (who has other Welsh associations), Frank Richards, and Siegfried Sassoon as well as David Jones and Wyn Griffith. Amongst poets particularly the tally is high: Edward Thomas and Wilfred Owen are two of the very few whose reputations

88. Richard Hughes and Raymond Garlick, 1974, after receiving, respectively, a Welsh Arts Council Major Award and a Poetry Prize for *A Sense of Time*

remain and increase from the First World War, and Alun Lewis is one of only two of that category from the Second. Since 1937 there has never been a time when one or more of the Anglo-Welsh poets discussed – Dylan Thomas, Vernon Watkins, David Jones, R.S. Thomas, for example – has not been widely recognised as of the highest rank. If at present that general recognition seems less extended than formerly, the change of direction – towards Wales rather than away from it – and the special circumstances of the last decade and a half may be held responsible.

For in reality the achievement continues. R.S. Thomas, with *H'm* (1972), *Laboratories of the Spirit* (1975), *Frequencies* (1978), *Between Here and Now* (1981) and *Later Poems* (1983), has moved the emphasis of his poetry from the depopulated countryside and a despairing nationalism towards the quest for the absent God, whose ground of being the modern reader is less familiar with. Leslie Norris, with the memory of a vanished Merthyr receding, keeps both his Sussex home and the very different ethos of the Teifi valley in his poetic consciousness: *Ransoms* (1970), *Mountains, Polecats, Pheasants* (1974) and *Water Voices* (1980), the last of which develops his experience of America, carry his varied evocations some way towards a more considerable reputation. His book of short stories, *Sliding* (1978), is, stylistically, a classic. Of Raymond Garlick's three latest collections, *A Sense of Europe* (1968) takes its bearings from his years in Holland, *A Sense of Time* (1972) involves him deeply with the trials of the nationalist young, and *Incense* (1976) shows him more tranquil on the shore of estuaried Llansteffan. If his "hope is still on what is to come", what he has already written is a sharp and heartening accompaniment to the decades since 1950. John Ormond, though there has been no new collection since *Definition of a Waterfall*,

89. Ruth Bidgood in the Camalch Valley, north Breconshire, 1967

90. Gillian Clarke, 1984

writes costively but in his best vein. And there are two talented newcomers of some seniority, both women. Ruth Bidgood, long absent from Wales, has found the solitudes of north Breconshire a setting to stimulate a historical imagination which inspires house and scene as much as person. *The Given Time* (1972), *Not Without Homage* (1975), *The Print of Miracle* (1978) and *Lighting Candles* (1982) have earned her a valued place in the concourse. Gillian Clarke, half a generation younger, is probably the poet, of them all, who by the exercise of her skills as a teacher and reader, has made her name most rapidly both in Wales and outside it. Beginning with the Triskel pamphlet *Snow on the Mountain* (1971), her poetry became widely popular with *The Sundial* (1978) and *Letter from a Far Country* (1982): her ability both to strike a distinctly feminine note and yet to evoke the spirit and tradition of the Welsh countryside in terms that are half-remembered as well as understood widens the appeal her work has for new readers of poetry as well as for the *literati*.

Attempts to put out an identikit picture of the Anglo-Welsh poet – which are all too often made and more frequently by foe than friend – never really succeed. Amongst the relatively senior poets just discussed there are as many differences as there are persons. A centrifugal pull affects them all, but the individual runs his circle as he wills.

In prose, it must be confessed, the conviction of achievement is less. There have been individual novels of real experimental quality like *Border Country* (1960) by Raymond Williams, one of the few significant and direction-setting critics of this generation. His *Second Generation* (1964), however, lost some of the original impetus and *The Fight for Manod* (1979), while choosing new ground, revealed more of the author's renewed feeling for Wales than of a deeper novelistic development. The last thirty years, however, have been enlivened by the work of a number of 'resident foreigners' like Oliver Onions, whose *Poor Man's Tapestry* (1946), perhaps the most unusual historical novel about Wales to date, won the James Tait Black Memorial Prize, Kingsley Amis, whose career as a novelist went off with a bang with *Lucky Jim* (1953) and *That Uncertain Feeling* (1955), and Peter Tinniswood, whose *Except You're a Bird* (1974) and other mordantly humorous works were successful enough to earn their transfer to television. John Cowper Powys (1872-1963), who in his later years came to

91. Raymond Williams at Oriel in 1980, after the publication of *The Fight for Manod*

92. John Cowper Powys and James Hanley at Eisteddfod Maldwyn, Corwen, May 1936, on
the day the former was admitted to the Gorsedd of Bards as Ioan Powys

live first at Corwen and then at Blaenau Ffestiniog, would never have agreed that he was not a Welshman, though his family's last connection with Wales was as far back as the sixteenth century. His two novels of Wales, *Owen Glendower* (1940) and *Porius* (1951), are in some respects brilliantly evocative but they were formed philosophically in his native Wessex: despite the enthusiasm with which he threw himself into Welsh history and contemporary controversy, his Wales was a country preconceived rather than observed and absorbed. *Maiden Castle* (1937) prefigures a great part of the Welsh mythology (as distinct from its Arthurian extensions) which John Cowper was to use later. James Hanley, for many years resident in Powys, wrote within a tighter compass: but the novels which began with *The Welsh Sonata* (1954), if thinly populated, were deeply and climactically written. The best-known incomer of all was undoubtedly Richard Hughes (1900-76), the gap in whose family connection with Wales was as long as that of John Cowper Powys. After a particularly precocious beginning at Charterhouse and Oxford, he disappeared into a period of unprivileged travel, to emerge in Wales, first at Laugharne and then, for the rest of his life, at Maentwrog. It is arguable whether such long residence made Welsh concerns so familiar that they could remain, unstressed, on the periphery of his world-picture or whether, after an early enthusiasm for the Portmadoc Players (for whom he wrote at least one play), they never did make much impact. Possibly, in any case, the innovative irony of *A High Wind in Jamaica* (1929), a work which reflects his footloose days, will last better than the more laboured history-into-fiction of his grand design, 'The Human Predicament', of which only two parts – *The Fox in the Attic* (1961) and *The Wooden Shepherdess* (1973) – were completed. Both these have their successful interludes but their characters succumb more and more to impersonality as scene follows scene on the historical backdrop. No account of the novel in English, however – and here the limitation of the Welsh context can be removed entirely – would be likely to omit Richard Hughes's name or that of John Cowper Powys.

Of recent years there have been enough 'native sons' in print to suggest that the economic difficulties which formerly beset the novel in Wales have largely disappeared. But high reputation here is still very restricted. Emyr Humphreys continues to extend the list of his works, and Alun Richards, after his moving and well-wrought novel *Home to an Empty House* (1973), has turned his attention to novels which, like Richard Hughes's *In Hazard* (1938), have the sea as an enclosing and determining factor. *Ennal's Point* (1977) and *Barque Whisper* (1979), the first two parts of a trilogy, are closely structured and markedly more subtle than is usual with stories of the sea. Against the contemporary belief in the uncommerciality of short stories, too, his *Dai Country* (1973) and *The Former Miss Merthyr Tydfil* (1976) were notable successes. But the older guard has been decimated by time and insufficiently replaced. Jack Jones died in 1970, Rhys Davies in 1978, Glyn Jones's last novel, *The Island of Apples*, appeared as long ago as 1965, and Gwyn Thomas, who died in 1981, devoted his last years to autobiography and stage plays. Henry Treece, whose reputation as a poet preceded the one he earned from the historical novels which began with *The Dark Island* (1952), died long before he was written out. Menna Gallie, who wrote three spirited novels – beginning with *Strike for a Kingdom* (1959) – never adequately followed them up. The stage emptied rapidly in the seventies and few of the new entrances have been firm and decisive. Alison Morgan has made one as a distinguished author of stories for children between ten and fifteen: from *Fish* (1971) to *Leaving*

Home (1979) and *Paul's Kite* (1981) she has shown an ability to use the stuff of ordinary living, without distortion or melodrama, to create a narrative for the younger reader. Stuart Evans, ever since *The Gardens of the Casino* (1976), has been making his way through the intellectually esoteric end of the market, and Sian James, with six novels to her credit, has devoted the one that is probably her best, *A Small Country* (1979), to the West Wales of her childhood. Alice Thomas Ellis, rather less Welsh than her pseudonym suggests, has earned high recognition from the critics for her four novels, each of which, from *The Sin Eater* (1977) to *The Other Side of the Fire* (1983), has been followed by greater applause. Among those who were, or are, less prolific, Goronwy Rees, whose autobiographical works are more distinguished than his novels, died in 1979, William Glynne-Jones in 1977, Cledwyn Hughes in 1978 and Tom Macdonald in 1980. W.H. Boore, Ron Berry, Alun Llewellyn, G.O. Jones, Aled Vaughan, John James, John L. Hughes and Moira Dearnley, each with a number of novels published, have not added to the tally recently, and the prose scene seems more thinly populated than it was. On the other hand, writers in a lighter genre – like Dick Francis and Leslie Thomas among the more established and Craig Thomas and Ken Follett among the newer arrivals – have been enjoying very considerable commercial success. Possibly some of the more innovative and distinguished books of the last two decades have been written outside the strictly creative field: Glyn Jones's *The Dragon Has Two Tongues* (1968), Ned Thomas's *The Welsh Extremist* (1971), George Ewart Evans's series of oral history compilations which runs from *Ask the Fellows who Cut the Hay* (1956) to *Horse Power and Magic* (1979), Raymond Williams's works of cultural history, *Culture and Society* (1958), *The Long Revolution* (1966) and *The Country and the City* (1973), and the more traditionally historical writing of Kenneth Morgan and Gwyn A. Williams, manifested in a number of recent books, have all marked new and distinctive peaks for writers in English from Wales.

XVII The Dramatic Tradition

The field of drama, even more than that of the novel, may suggest some truth in the traditional adage that the Welshman is short of puff. Most amateur players and playgoers are still familiar with *The Poacher* (1914) and *Birds of a Feather* (1927), amongst the one-act plays of J.O. Francis, as with Ronald Elwy Mitchell's *A Husband for Breakfast* (1937), D.T. Davies's *Pancakes* (1960) – though this is a translation from the Welsh – and the Davy Jones one-acters of T.C. Thomas, which appeared from 1955. This is a field in which Wales's amateur tradition has meant that good writing and popular appreciation have been better able to coincide than elsewhere. But what promised, from about 1912 onwards until the outbreak of the Second World War, to become a substantial tradition of full-length drama for the stage (in which the amateur tradition could be of relatively little assistance), fatally lost impetus thereafter. J.O Francis's *Change* (1913), still too little regarded, was the first harbinger of this promise: his *The Dark Little People* (1922) and *Cross Currents* (1923) from South Wales combined with Richard Hughes's *A Comedy of Good and Evil* (1924) from North and Caradoc Evans's shouted-down *Taffy* (1923) from London to suggest that a varied and interesting movement was on its way. Caradoc's vitriol and Hughes's *grand-guignol* were in no sense ordinary. The arrival of Emlyn Williams and his work on the London stage appeared to indicate a movement away from satire, if not from violence: *Night Must Fall* (1935) and *The Corn is Green* (1938) (the latter based on his boyhood experience in Flintshire) brought Welsh drama nearer the middle of the road and into the thick of the plaudits of fashion. It is no less than fair to indicate that the latter play may be timed in closely with the special interest in Wales generated by Dylan Thomas

93. J.O. Francis. Portrait by Ceri Richards

and the Anglo-Welsh writers of the 'first movement'. But all this promised more than was afterwards performed: Emlyn Williams's later plays, with the exception of *The Wind of Heaven* (1945), lacked either what Matthew Arnold called 'high seriousness', a sufficient poetry, or the comic inventiveness which could maintain the engagement of a public already tiring of Welsh eccentricities.

Since then only Eynon Evans, who began with *Affairs of Bryngolau* (1936) but achieved his greatest successes with *Wishing Well* (1946) and *Bless this House* (1954), and Gwyn Thomas have achieved any degree of public attention. Eynon Evans's work succeeds reasonably well at the level of entertainment: Gwyn Thomas's, in failing more than occasionally to do that, is nevertheless aiming much higher. *The Keep* (1962), for instance, demonstrates Thomas's almost unlimited fund of wit against a serious failure to create separate characters or any satisfactory movement of plot: the author's gifts appear as those of an unrivalled *raconteur* who multiplies himself as the different players walk on. In the novels the style carries this: on the stage the characters too often participate in the kind of one-voice talking- shop that Shaw sometimes produced. Gwyn Thomas's other plays reinforce this impression, even the last of them, *The Breakers* (1976): their aura is recognised as unmistakably Welsh, whatever claims the playwright continued to make for them as 'mongrel', but they adapt badly to the needs of the stage.

There have been one or two valuable plays of ideas in recent years, like Ewart Alexander's *Buzz Buzz Critch Critch* (1969), but they have rarely been widely performed. Indeed, much of the drama that takes itself seriously – the plays of Alun Richards and Alun Owen may be instanced here – has suffered from the weakening of class and social attitudes against which a full-length play can hope to measure itself. Two other generalisations may be made: the more political theatre which has become

94. Emlyn Williams and Sybil Thorndike
in *The Corn is Green*, 1978

95. A still from Gwyn Thomas's play,
The Keep, 1960

popular in England in the last two decades has not attracted Welsh playwrights, and the diversion of dramatic energy into the shorter vehicles offered by television has been more successful proportionately in Wales than in England, most of all since there have been three channels to accommodate it.

Possibly the balance of this situation is about to change. Until 1975 there was no theatre circuit in Wales of a size to suggest that a play on a Welsh theme in English had a chance of commercial viability, and this during a period when the *prima facie* interest of Welsh themes in London had greatly diminished. During the last decade several training schemes have been inaugurated in the attempt to produce home-grown dramatists, and the emergence of drama companies like Made in Wales is some assurance that these policies are bearing fruit. As yet, however, no single writer of sufficient reputation has appeared to personalise this development.

For the time being established playwrights like Alun Owen, Alun Richards and Ewart Alexander are able, to whatever extent they may wish, to turn their talents to script-writing for television and radio. Others, like the late Elwyn Jones of the 'Softly, Softly' series and Elaine Morgan, who has some distinguished scripts to her credit, have specialised from the beginning in work for television. From an adaptation like that of *How Green Was My Valley* to the dramatisation of a historical episode like *The Burston School Strike* the latter has shown herself in the front rank of her craft. She has, in addition, written books such as *The Descent of Woman* (1974), of which the feminist movement has made a considerable commercial success.

XVIII Present Tense

Television, less ephemeral in its impact since the development of video cassettes, is, for all that, unable as yet to build reputations as books do. Long-term renown probably lies, for the foreseeable future, where commercial success does not, in the field of poetry. It is here that Welsh writers in English, as tradition would lead one to expect, have been pre-eminent. But justice has not yet been done to the younger figures in this tradition who, if less numerous than the total health of Anglo-Welsh literature would require, nevertheless demand attention. There are a few, like Gloria Evans Davies, Joyce Herbert and Peter Preece, who have written only intermittently because of ill-health, others, like Peter Finch and John Idris Jones, who have written less because of their involvement in the selling or publishing of books, and a few more again, like Sam Adams (whose work as an editor has been considerable), Meic Stephens (vastly occupied for eight years as editor of *The Oxford Companion to the Literature of Wales*) and possibly Douglas Phillips, Alan Perry and John Pook, for whom the trammels of professional responsibility have been too great. There are, too, before the central group of younger poets is considered, a few who have earned the title *Anglo-Welsh* by their contribution over years to English writing in Wales, most notably Jeremy Hooker and J.P. Ward, but also including names newer to the public like those of Nigel Wells, Bryan Aspden and Jean Earle (the last of whom has begun to build a reputation when past seventy). Of Christine Furnival, who might have been included in this group, little has been heard recently.

No generalisation will serve to describe the most active of the younger poets, but perhaps the characteristic most widely shared among them is a greater degree of realism, of attention to society as it is, than was common to their elders. Any lament for the loss of Welshness is, inevitably, muted: instead there is an examination of the detritus, of the habits, new and old, of the evolving population, and an attempt at definition of the poet's own place in the continuing evolution. Tony Curtis and Robert Minhinnick, for example, have written most effectively of all upon their roots, on the

96. Tony Curtis, drawing by Alan Salisbury, 1985

97. Nigel Jenkins, July 1983

98. Robert Minhinnick: Welsh Arts Council
Prizewinner, 1984, for *Life Sentences*

relationship of what they remember with what is, the one in the context of Pembrokeshire, the other in that of Glamorgan, though the rest of their interests differ considerably. One of the latest poets to appear, Christopher Meredith, is seeking to relate his upbringing in Tredegar to a very different rural Wales. Others, like Mike Jenkins and Graham Thomas, examine the places where they live, Merthyr and Abertillery respectively, with sympathy but also with a kind of unsentimental precision, uncovering the history that is relevant. A little apart, perhaps, stand Nigel Jenkins, the overtones of whose work are more generally political, and John Davies, who, after evoking the local Prestatyn scene, has begun to write more obliquely and personally. Christine Evans from Llŷn, another new arrival, aligns herself largely with the realist approach. Duncan Bush, on the other hand, though by no means the only younger poet with a more cosmopolitan experience, has not indicated the same concentration of interest, and Sheenagh Pugh's work clearly rejects the immediate and draws inspiration from more literary sources. It is too early to say what the poetic stature of any individual in this group may prove to be. What can be discerned is a considerable identity of style: with the exception of Sheenagh Pugh and possibly that of Robert Minhinnick these younger poets are much less interested than their elders in poetic structure and tension within the line: on the other hand, intellectual content and the development of meaning are usually matters of close attention.

It is not the achievement of these poets that is arguable: it is the point in the social history of Wales at which, not of their own volition, they now find themselves, and whether the terminology that has been used so far in this literary history can continue much longer to be applicable. Is Anglo-Welsh writing, in any meaningful sense of that term, likely to survive the century?

Obviously, very few among the poets named in the paragraphs latest above are now writing for and to a linguistically *Welsh* situation. For the most part they come from that majority of the population of Wales which is no longer, except very occasionally, in touch with the Welsh language: they are therefore unaware of and unattracted by the values of the Welsh tradition, which itself, of course, is changing. This does not make them unpatriotic, in the sense that they no longer see Wales as a distinct social and cultural entity (though that may be true of a few): they are bound to be influenced by being part of a small geographical unit (which claims to be a good deal more than that) and an even smaller literary community. To that extent, they are likely to identify more closely with Wales than all but a very few English poets do with their native region – one thinks here of Norman Nicholson at Millom or Ted Hughes and the mark of Yorkshire on him as the sorts of exception comparable – and it may be that that situation will persist for the foreseeable future. What is in question here is the continuing applicability of the term *Anglo-Welsh*. In its wider meaning, as describing the work of a writer born in Wales but writing in English, its validity is bound to continue in some sort, but insofar as there is in it an implied point of reference to the Welsh language its usefulness diminishes. Many of the younger Anglo-Welsh writers have not been affected by any literary tradition other than the English and a minority of them only seeks an alignment with Welsh history. In this respect the last decades of the twentieth century must be distinguished from the whole of the period before 1900, during which Anglo-Welsh writing, however 'English' some of it may have been, had to take account of a predominantly Welsh-speaking Wales, even if the intent was deliberately or snobbishly to ignore it. There is a difference between *ignoring* and *being ignorant of*, and although it might be held, on the one hand, that the sheer quantity of information about Wales made available by the media in the present makes ignorance impossible, it is even more true that the information supplied about Wales *and* the wider world is in total so enormous that even an intelligent hearer or reader must needs choose what small portion of it to assimilate. In consequence, a writer separated genealogically, geographically or emotionally from the much smaller existing area of 'Welshness' need never choose consciously for or against it. If it is in his mind at all, it may be no more than a marginal concern. In these new conditions the use of the term *Anglo-Welsh* as descriptive, in any real sense, of writers born within Wales's boundaries but separated willy-nilly from the Welsh language and tradition has a diminishing usefulness.

Anglo-Welsh writers of 'the first' and 'second movements' were rarely in this totally anglicised position – 'the first', because most of them, involuntarily or otherwise, had an acquaintance with the then receding Welsh language and the different culture that had flourished within it, 'the second', because many of them had made a personal commitment to the re-creation of the link between Welsh culture and language and writing in English. Generalisations about this, however, are necessarily fraught with danger. All through the twentieth century there have been a few writers from Wales who have been little involved, if at all, with a culture based on the Welsh language: what becomes plain is that, as generation succeeds generation in south-east Wales and other areas of the country from which the Welsh language has largely receded, writers are bound to develop, from what is an overwhelming majority of the population, whose natal and emotional circumstances require of them no comment upon a *Welsh* situation because that situation is not in any real sense theirs. Indeed, as one contemplates the attempt in these pages to give shape to the development of Anglo-Welsh writing, a consciousness grows, as the century wears on, that the term *Anglo-*

Welsh is being used in two distinct ways and yet without sufficient differentiation. It is a purely geographical label, of which the validity in some sort remains. It is also, and much more exactly, descriptive of those writers who, chiefly in 'the second movement', have sought to bring writing in English into direct and fruitful contact with the Welsh literacy and historic tradition. This duality of application is unfortunate and confusing: if, diagrammatically, it may be seen to resemble a small circle within a larger one, there is still a looseness of thinking about it which fails to explain why the work of an English-born poet like Raymond Garlick brings him within the narrower circle although he could not qualify for the wider.

It is, however, the survival of this narrower circle that is mainly in question. The wider, even if its label appears less and less appropriate, must needs survive because writers in English will, by the law of averages, continue to appear in Wales.

What, then, are the chances that the narrower category of Anglo-Welsh writing will continue? Undoubtedly the Welsh situation has altered markedly since 1965, when the latest of the older writers emerged. The Welsh language is now receding slowly, if at all, in terms of the total numbers speaking it: but this relative standstill disguises a continued weakening in certain rural areas and balances against it increases in city and urban areas, mainly brought about by the new secondary schools that teach through Welsh and the popularity of language classes amongst adults. Some of the youthful energy that might have gone into writing in English in the highly populated districts has been turned towards the learning of the Welsh language and there is a widespread attempt to create a strictly modern 'Welshness' which ignores old shibboleths like the values of Nonconformity and the closeness of the rural community. This new situation leaves the young writer who, for whatever reason, has not chosen to opt into Welsh, more separated from 'Welshness' than his predecessors were because the shibboleth is now almost solely that of the language. Not having that, he is much more completely shut out from the Welsh world than if there were, as there once was, a recognisably different lifestyle to attract him. Gone is the nostalgic regret, as well as the guilt, that possessed an older generation separated from its Welsh roots. It is now as true that Welsh language culture has moved away from that poor but romantic past as that English language culture has rejected it.

One possibility remains. It may be that a significant number of 'Welsh learners', discovering the urge to write, will realise that their linguistic powers do not permit them to reach the demanding standard that they envisage by means of and in a second language – that they will, in short, learn from experience that the only language in which their education has permitted them to be creative is English. Such writers would be in a position to bring back into English some of the feeling, the different values, hopes and expectations that they had begun to understand in Welsh. This is not, perhaps, exactly the way in which Nigel Jenkins, Mike Jenkins and Christopher Meredith have built their bridges across the linguistic divide: all of them learned Welsh as a personal decision *after* their schooldays. It remains to be seen whether there are younger writers still, educated much more completely and for longer in Welsh, who, for whatever reason, will feel unable to follow the example of Bobi Jones but will, although deeply impregnated with a more modern 'Welshness', fall back upon the English prop of which they are more certain. If this happens, there will again be writers who are 'Anglo-Welsh' in the strictest sense. It could happen, and the tradition would then be extended beyond the century. But it has not happened yet.

Bibliography

Critical and General:

W.J. Hughes, *Wales and the Welsh in English Literature* (from Shakespeare to Scott). (Hughes & Son, Wrexham, 1924).

Raymond Garlick, *An Introduction to Anglo-Welsh Literature* (University of Wales Press, 1970).

Brynmor Jones, *A Bibliography of Anglo-Welsh Literature 1900-1965* (Wales & Monmouthshire Branch of the Library Association, 1970).

Sam Adams & Gwilym Rees Hughes, *Triskel One: Essays on Welsh and Anglo-Welsh Literature* (Christopher Davies, 1971). *Triskel Two* (1973).

R. Brinley Jones, ed., *Anatomy of Wales* (Gwerin Publications, 1972). *Vide* Roland Mathias, 'Thin Spring and Tributary: Welshmen Writing in English'.

Meic Stephens, ed., *The Arts in Wales 1950-75* (Welsh Arts Council, 1979). *Vide* Roland Mathias, 'Literature in English'.

Anthony Conran, *The Cost of Strangeness: Essays on the English Poets of Wales* (Gwasg Gomer, 1982).

Roland Mathias, *A Ride Through the Wood* (Studies of David Jones, Dylan Thomas, Alun Lewis, R.S. Thomas etc.) (Poetry Wales Press, 1985).

Biographies in *The Writers of Wales Series*

ed. Meic Stephens and R. Brinley Jones (University of Wales Press):

Alan Rudrum, *Henry Vaughan* (1981)
Belinda Humfrey, *John Dyer* (1980)
Peter W. Trinder, *Mrs. Hemans* (1984)
Douglas Phillips, *Sir Lewis Morris* (1981)
Sally Jones, *Allen Raine* (1979)
J. Kimberley Roberts, *Ernest Rhys* (1983)
D.P.M. Michael, *Arthur Machen* (1971)
Lawrence Hockey, *W.H. Davies* (1971)
Jeremy Hooker, *John Cowper Powys* (1973)
R. George Thomas, *Edward Thomas* (1972)
T.L. Williams, *Caradoc Evans* (1970)
Keri Edwards, *Jack Jones* (1974)
Greg Hill, *Llewelyn Wyn Griffith* (1984)
Christopher W. Newman, *Hilda Vaughan* (1981)
René Hague, *David Jones* (1975)
David Smith, *Lewis Jones* (1982)
Peter Thomas, *Richard Hughes* (1973)
Sam Adams, *Geraint Goodwin* (1975)
David Rees, *Rhys Davies* (1975)
Tony Bianchi, *Richard Vaughan* (1984)
Leslie Norris, *Glyn Jones* (1973)
Islwyn Jenkins, *Idris Davies* (1972)
Don Dale-Jones, *Emlyn Williams* (1979)
Roland Mathias, *Vernon Watkins* (1974)
Cecil Price, *Gwyn Jones* (1976)
Moira Dearnley, *Margiad Evans* (1982)

Ian Michael, *Gwyn Thomas* (1977)
W. Moelwyn Merchant, *R.S. Thomas* (1979)
Walford Davies, *Dylan Thomas* (1972)
Alun John, *Alun Lewis* (1970)
Ioan Williams, *Emyr Humphreys* (1980)
Julian Croft, *T.H. Jones* (1976)
J.P. Ward, *Raymond Williams* (1984)
Tony Curtis, *Dannie Abse* (1985)

Other Biographies (selected):

Meic Stephens, ed. *Artists in Wales* (Gwasg Gomer). Vol.I 1971: Vol.II 1973: Vol.III 1977.
R.George Thomas, *Edward Thomas: A Portrait* (Clarendon Press, 1985).
Paul Ferris, *Dylan Thomas* (Hodder & Stoughton, 1977).
John Pikoulis, *Alun Lewis: A Life* (Poetry Wales Press, 1984).

Anthologies of Anglo-Welsh Poetry:

Elizabeth A. Sharp, ed., *Lyra Celtica* (Patrick Geddes, 1896). Includes two sections: (a) Early Cymric and Mediaeval Welsh and (b) Contemporary Anglo-Celtic Poets (Wales).
A.G. Prys-Jones, ed., *Welsh Poets* (Erskine Macdonald, 1917). The first anthology devoted entirely to Anglo-Welsh verse.Grace Rhys, ed., *A Celtic Anthology* (Harrap, 1927), Includes one section of 94 pages devoted to Welsh verse in translation *and* Anglo-Welsh verse.
Keidrich Rhys, ed., *Modern Welsh Poetry* (Faber, 1944). Despite the title, an entirely Anglo-Welsh selection.
Bryn Griffiths, ed., *Welsh Voices* (Dent, 1967). An anthology of *new* Anglo-Welsh verse.
Gerald Morgan ed., *This World of Wales* (University of Wales Press, 1968). Anglo-Welsh verse from the seventeenth to the twentieth century.
John Stuart Williams and Meic Stephens, eds., *The Lilting House* (Christopher Davies / Dent, 1969). Anglo-Welsh verse 1917-67.
Sam Adams, ed., *Ten Anglo-Welsh Poets* (Carcanet Press, 1974).
Roland Mathias, ed., *Sixteen Welsh Poets* A Special Issue of *Spirit*, Seton Hall University, U.S.A., 1974.
Don Dale-Jones & Randal Jenkins, eds., *Twelve Modern Anglo-Welsh Poets* (University of London Press, 1975).
Gwyn Jones, ed., *The Oxford Book of Welsh Verse in English* (Oxford University Press, 1977). Includes many translations from the Welsh.Meic Stephens & Peter Finch, eds., *Green Horse* (Christopher Davies, 1978). An anthology of the work of younger Anglo-Welsh poets.
Dora Polk, ed., *A Book Called Hiraeth* (Alun Books, 1982). Poetry and prose, with many translations from the Welsh, embodying various aspects of *hiraeth*.
Dannies Abse, ed., *Wales in Verse* (Secker & Warburg, 1983). An anthology with a topographical emphasis.
Raymond Garlick & Roland Mathias, eds., *Anglo-Welsh Poetry 1480-1980* (Poetry Wales Press, 1984). The most complete anthology thus far.Susan Butler, ed., *Common Ground: Poets in a Welsh Landscape* (Poetry Wales Press, 1985). Seven poets: each poem with a photograph in face.

Anthologies of Anglo-Welsh Poetry with a Regional Emphasis:

Tony Curtis, ed., *Pembrokeshire Poets* (E.A. Roberts, Llanychaer, 1975).
W. Rhys Nicholas, ed., *Triangle: An Anthology of Poems from the South-West* (West Wales Association for the Arts, 1977).
John Davies & John Pook, eds., *Here in North Wales* (Clwyd Centre for Educational Technology, 1982). Prose as well as poetry.
John Davies & Mike Jenkins, *The Valleys* (Poetry Wales Press, 1984). Poetry *and* prose.

Anthologies intended for Schools:

Sam Adams & Gwilym Rees Hughes, eds., *Dragon's Hoard* (Gwasg Gomer, 1976). For older pupils.
Don Dale-Jones & Randal Jenkins, eds., *Wales Today* (Gwasg Gomer, 1976). Poems and pictures.

Annual (later biennial) Anthologies of Anglo-Welsh Verse

John Stuart Williams, ed., *Poems '69*.
Wyn Binding, ed., *Poems '70*.
Jeremy Hooker, ed., *Poems '71*.
John Ackerman, ed., *Poems '72*.
Gwyn Ramage, ed., *Poems '73*.
Peter Elfed Lewis, ed., *Poems '74*.
Glyn Jones, ed., *Poems '76*.
Graham Allen, ed., *Poems '78*.
(all Gwasg Gomer)

Collected Poems by individual Poets

(a few recent editions):

Alan Rudrum, ed., *Henry Vaughan: The Complete Poems* (Penguin Books, 1976).
Daniel George, ed., *The Complete Poems of W.H. Davies* (Cape, 1963).
David Jones, *The Sleeping Lord and Other Fragments* (late poems) (Faber 1974).
Glyn Jones, *Selected Poems* (Gwasg Gomer, 1975).
Islwyn Jenkins, ed., *The Collected Poems of Idris Davies* (Gwasg Gomer, 1972).
Vernon Watkins, *Unity of the Stream* (a new selection by Gwen Watkins and Roland Mathias) (Gwasg Gomer, for Yr Academi Gymreig, 1978).
R.S. Thomas, *Song at the Year's Turning* (selected early poems) (Hart-Davis, 1956).
Dylan Thomas, *Collected Poems 1934-1952* (Dent, 1952)
Jeremy Hooker & Gweno Lewis, eds., *Selected Poems of Alun Lewis* (Unwin Paperbacks, 1981).
Roland Mathias, *Burning Brambles: Selected Poems 1944-1979* (Gwasg Gomer, 1983)
Julian Croft and Don Dale-Jones, ed., *The Collected Poems of T. Harri Jones* (Gwas Gomer, 1977).
Dannie Abse, *Collected Poems 1948-76* (Hutchinson, 1977).
John Tripp, *Collected Poems 1958-78* (Christopher Davies, 1978).

Anthologies of Anglo-Welsh Short Stories:

Elizabeth Inglis Jones and others, eds., *Welsh Short Stories* (Faber, 1937).
Gwyn Jones, ed., *Welsh Short Stories* (Penguin Books, 1941).
George Ewart Evans, ed., *Welsh Short Stories* (Faber, 1959).
Sam Adams & Roland Mathias, eds., *The Shining Pyramid and Other Stories* (Gwasg Gomer, 1970).
Gwyn Jones & Islwyn Ffowc Elis, eds., *Twenty-Five Welsh Short Stories* (Oxford University Press, 1971).
Lynn Hughes, ed., *The Old Man of the Mist* (Martin, Brian & O'Keeffe, 1974). New writing.
Alun Richards, *The Penguin Book of Welsh Short Stories* (Penguin Books, 1976).

Collected Stories by individual authors:

(a few recent editions);

Sam Adams & Roland Mathias, *The Collected Short Stories of Geraint Goodwin* (H.G. Walters, Tenby, 1976).
Glyn Jones, *Selected Short Stories* (Dent, 1971).
Gwyn Jones, *Selected Short Stories* (Oxford University Press, 1974).
Dylan Thomas, *The Collected Stories* (Everyman Paperback, 1983).
Gwyn Thomas, *Selected Short Stories* (Poetry Wales Press, 1984).
Leslie Norris, *Sliding* (Dent, 1978).
Alun Richards, *Dai Country* (1974) and The Former Miss Merthyr Tydfil (1976) (both Michael Joseph).

Anglo-Welsh Literary Magazines (from 1937):

Wales (ed. Keidrych Rhys 1937-59, with two intermissions).
The Welsh Review (ed. Gwyn Jones 1939-49, with one intermission).
Dock Leaves (1949-57), subsequently *The Anglo-Welsh Review* (1957-) (ed. Raymond Garlick 1949-60, Roland Mathias 1961-76, Gillian Clarke 1976-84, Greg Hill 1984- .
Poetry Wales (1965-) (ed. Meic Stephens 1965-67, Gerald Morgan 1967-68, Meic Stephens 1969-73, Sam Adams 1973-76, J.P. Ward 1976-80, Cary Archard 1980-86, Mike Jenkins 1986-).
Second Aeon (ed. Peter Finch 1967-74).
Planet (1970-80 and 1985-) (ed. Ned Thomas, Sara Erskine, John Tripp, 1970-80: John Barnie 1985-).
Arcade (1980-81) (ed. John Osmond, Nigel Jenkins).

Acknowledgements for Photographs

The following are gratefully acknowledged for their permission to use the photographs which make up this book:

Ashmolean Museum, Oxford, 8; Ruth Bidgood 89; Bodleian Library, Oxford, 3; BBC, 77; BBC Hulton Picture Library, 37; British Library, 11, 26; Susan Butler, 90; Cardiff Central Library, 14, 27; Carmarthen Museum, 36; Tony Curtis, 97; Glynn Vivian Art Gallery, Swansea, 28, 60; Mrs. R. Goodwin, 67; Susan Griggs Agency, 95; House of Lords Record Office, 4; Dr. Daniel Jones, 58; Dr. Glyn Jones, 55, 62, 63, 71; Mrs. Gweno Lewis, 69; The Raymond Mander & Joe Mitcheson Theatre Collection, 94; Roland Mathias, 44, 59, 79, 82, 92; Robert Morgan, 80; Eben. Morris, 48; National Film Institute, 64; National Library of Wales, 6, 9, 12, 16, 17, 19, 21, 24, 25, 29, 30, 33, 34, 35, 39, 42, 43, 45, 46, 50, 52, 56, 70, 78, 93; National Museum of Wales, 10, 20, 22, 23, 32, 49, 72; National Portrait Gallery, 31, 40; Newport Library, 51; *Newcastle Herald* 66; John Ormond, 83; A.G. Prys-Jones, 54; R.C.A.M. (Wales), 7, 41; Headmaster, Ruthin Grammar School, 5; Mrs. Myfanwy Thomas, 53; University College, Cardiff, 15, 18, 38, 47; Mrs. Hilda Vaughan, 65; Ian Walker, 85; Richard Watkins, 86; The Watkins Family, 68; Welsh Arts Council, 73, 74, 75, 84, 88, 91, 96, 98.

Index